THE PSYCHOLOGY OF WEATHER

Do you feel happier on a sunny day? Are you afraid of thunderstorms? Are you dreaming of a white Christmas?

The Psychology of Weather explores our relationship with the weather, and how it can affect our mood, behaviour, and lifestyle. The book sheds light on our preoccupation with this natural phenomenon, providing insights into how the weather on the day we were born can directly affect our intelligence and personality, and exploring such surprising findings that suicide rates peak in the spring and summer.

When the weather affects everything from our buying behaviour to the jobs we do, *The Psychology of Weather* shows us that understanding and appreciating the weather can improve our well-being and contribute to human survival.

Trevor Harley is Emeritus Professor of Psychology at the University of Dundee. Following a lifelong interest in weather, Trevor now researches at the intersection of psychology and weather, considering himself a psychometeorologist.

THE PSYCHOLOGY OF EVERYTHING

The Psychology of Everything is a series of books which debunk the myths and pseudo-science surrounding some of life's biggest questions.

The series explores the hidden psychological factors that drive us, from our sub-conscious desires and aversions, to the innate social instincts handed to us across the generations. Accessible, informative, and always intriguing, each book is written by an expert in the field, examining how research-based knowledge compares with popular wisdom, and illustrating the potential of psychology to enrich our understanding of humanity and modern life.

Applying a psychological lens to an array of topics and contemporary concerns – from sex to addiction to conspiracy theories – The Psychology of Everything will make you look at everything in a new way.

Titles in the series:

The Psychology of Grief
Richard Gross

The Psychology of Sex
Meg-John Barker

The Psychology of Dieting
Jane Ogden

The Psychology of Performance
Stewart T. Cotterill

The Psychology of Trust
Ken J. Rotenberg

The Psychology of Working Life
Toon Taris

The Psychology of Conspiracy Theories
Jan-Willem van Prooijen

The Psychology of Addiction
Jenny Svanberg

The Psychology of Fashion
Carolyn Mair

The Psychology of Gardening
Harriet Gross

The Psychology of Gender
Gary W. Wood

The Psychology of Climate Change
Geoffrey Beattie

The Psychology of Vampires
David Cohen

The Psychology of Chess
Fernand Gobet

The Psychology of Music
Susan Hallam

The Psychology of Retirement
Doreen Rosenthal and Susan M. Moore

The Psychology of Weather
Trevor Harley

The Psychology of School Bullying
Peter Smith

The Psychology of Driving
Graham J. Hole

The Psychology of Celebrity
Gayle Stever

For further information about this series please visit:
www.thepsychologyofeverything.co.uk

THE PSYCHOLOGY OF WEATHER

TREVOR HARLEY

Routledge
Taylor & Francis Group

LONDON AND NEW YORK

First published 2019
by Routledge
4 Park Square, Milton Park, Abingdon, Oxon OX14 4RN

and by Routledge
605 Third Avenue, New York, NY 10017

Routledge is an imprint of the Taylor & Francis Group, an informa business

British Library Cataloguing-in-Publication Data
A catalogue record for this book is available from the British Library

Library of Congress Cataloging-in-Publication Data
Names: Harley, Trevor A., author.
Title: The psychology of weather / Trevor Harley.
Description: 1 Edition. | New York : Routledge, 2019.
Identifiers: LCCN 2018024221 (print) | LCCN 2018035415 (ebook) |
    ISBN 9781351185042 (Adobe) | ISBN 9781351185035 (ePub) |
    ISBN 9781351185028 (Mobipocket) | ISBN 9780815394846
    (hardback) | ISBN 9780815394877 (pbk.) | ISBN 9781351185059
    (ebook)
Subjects: LCSH: Psychology. | Weather.
Classification: LCC BF121 (ebook) | LCC BF121 .H2277 2019
    (print) | DDC 150—dc23
LC record available at https://lccn.loc.gov/2018024221

ISBN: 978-0-8153-9484-6 (hbk)
ISBN: 978-0-8153-9487-7 (pbk)
ISBN: 978-1-351-18505-9 (ebk)

Typeset in Joanna
by Apex CoVantage, LLC

CONTENTS

Preface   ix

1   Weather and mood   1

2   Weather and health   19

3   Weather and behaviour   35

4   Weather and belief   53

5   Weather and society   71

Further reading   91

PREFACE

It might not be immediately obvious what psychology has to do with the weather, but a little thought suggests that there is some relationship. Is it sunny and warm outside? Could those factors be contributing to your amazing sense of well-being? Or is it dull and wet? Could that be why you feel a bit down today? Are you putting a bit more effort into clearing that pile of jobs because the weather is grim and there's nothing better to do? Is it the depths of winter and you haven't seen the sun for several days? Could that be why you have been feeling so glum for the last few weeks? Is there a thunderstorm forecast? Could the storm be related to your headache that's been building for a few hours? You were born at the height of a great summer? Is that why you have a sunny and warm disposition? And why did you ignore that severe weather warning this morning, so going too fast and skidding on the ice and then denting your bumper? We have evolved in conjunction with what is happening in nature, so it would not be that surprising if our climate and weather had some effect on our mood and behaviour.

It sounds very plausible that good weather makes us happy and bad weather makes us depressed, and many people have the belief that we are so affected, but is there any evidence for this state of affairs? It's remarkably difficult to come across clear summaries of the many experimental findings that are accessible to laypeople, and this book fills that gap. The literature is large, confusing, and often contradictory, but I hope this book can make some sense of it.

Looking at psychology and the weather is also an excellent means of finding out about what psychology can do when applied to a real-world problem, and the many studies exemplify the difficulties of exploring what might be quite small effects in the population at large. As is often remarked, many psychology findings are based on university students aged 18–21, which means that we can control the conditions in our experiments, but have to be optimistic about being able to generalise our results to the wider population. With psychology and the weather we have the world's population to consider, and we cannot control the conditions in nature as we can in the laboratory; we cannot at will (yet) make it snow in Johannesburg while creating a winter heatwave in Vladivostok.

We should not forget that the weather is a beautiful and fascinating natural phenomenon. It is easy to be glib about the weather, yet few natural phenomena impact on so many of us with such variation, and often, if we can stand back a bit, such grandeur and beauty. Look, really look, at a rainbow, or open your eyes and ears to a thunderstorm. No wonder these phenomena are so strongly embedded in our psyche and our cultural history. No wonder that the weather can affect us so profoundly.

I am very grateful to Routledge and particularly to my editor, Ceri McLardy, for giving me the opportunity to write this book. May the sun shine on her overseas vacations for years to come. The book is one of a series called *The Psychology of Everything*, and in that series this book stands out as one whose title ends up lacking grammatically. Silverley Allen went through the final manuscript and spotted numerous errors and made many helpful suggestions; may it rain only when you are asleep or indoors. And finally, as ever, for Siobhan: you are the sunshine of my life.

Trevor Harley

Emeritus Professor of Psychology, University of Dundee

trevor.harley@mac.com

www.trevorharley.com

May 2018

1

WEATHER AND MOOD

INTRODUCTION

Psychology and the weather? How on earth do these things go together?

The weather affects much of what we do. It determines what food we can eat, and not so long ago whether there was food we could eat at all, whether there is water for drinking, growing crops, raising animals, and cleaning readily available, whether we are likely to be inside or outside, and how comfortable we feel. Air conditioning is only a recent invention, and of course is still unavailable in much of the world. Life and civilisation could develop on Earth only because the temperature, the amount of water, and the composition of the atmosphere lay within certain happy values. Weather affects us profoundly; it is a matter of life and death, and so it shouldn't be surprising that it has an enormous role in our lives. As psychology is the science of why we behave as we do, it is then only natural that psychologists should be concerned with the weather and how it affects our behaviour. On reflection the only surprise is that psychologists haven't been more concerned with the weather.

The weather might affect us in more subtle but still important ways. When it is a warm sunny spring day, we believe our souls sing, so we hurry outside, and according to Alfred, Lord Tennyson, in his poem "Locksley Hall", "a young man's fancy lightly turns to thoughts of love". As winter deepens we feel gloom descend upon us, and we sit shivering in the darkness, depressed and yearning for summer. Or at least many of us think we do. Does the weather really affect our mood and our everyday behaviour? Does it affect mental illness – are we more likely to be seriously depressed when the weather is dull and gloomy? Are children born in summer at an advantage? Surprisingly little is known in answer to these and other questions; this book tries to answer them.

SCIENCE, PSYCHOLOGY, AND THE WEATHER

The weather interacts with psychology in three ways. First, there's how the weather affects us. Second, there's what our beliefs about the weather reveal about us. And finally when we come to study the influence of the weather on us, the weather provides an excellent environment for how to do psychology.

Often to the surprise of a first-year student, psychology is a science, and mostly an experimental science. In hot summers murder rates and ice cream sales both increase. Does one cause another? Do some people become psychotic killers after eating a vanilla and strawberry cone? That explanation sounds rather unlikely, but clearly there is something to be explained. This finding is an example of a correlation: as one thing changes, so does another. But, as we are fond of repeating to our students, a correlation by no means implies causation: it – probably – isn't the ice cream sales causing the murder rate to go up (or vice versa – a satisfied murderer reaches for an ice cream cone). In this example it's quickly apparent that a third variable, high temperature, is responsible for the increase in both ice cream sales and incidence of violence. A moment's more reflection suggests that perhaps it isn't even necessarily the high temperature that's responsible; maybe it's some other variable correlated with high temperature, such as excessive sunshine, or people getting sunburned and becoming irritable and on a short fuse, or high humidity plus high temperature, or even some other hidden variable that we can't immediately imagine. Just observing stuff makes it difficult to work out what is causing something; for that, we need to carry out controlled experiments.

In a psychology experiment we assign participants randomly to experimental groups, and we try to keep as much as possible constant except for the experimental manipulation of interest. That way we can draw conclusions about causation with confidence. Suppose we kept one large group of randomly selected people in a very hot room and another similar group of people in an identical room but at a low temperature. We leave them alone for half an hour and then come back and find that the people in the cold room are talking away amicably to each other, while everyone in the hot room is fighting, or even worse, a couple of people have been murdered. We might then reasonably conclude that higher temperatures make us more aggressive, particularly if we can repeat or *replicate* this finding several times.

Unfortunately the weather doesn't lend itself to being involved in controlled experiments because we can't, as yet anyway, manipulate it directly reliably. We can't make it hot and sunny in one place one day and then cold and dull the next (and even if we could we would have to be careful with our conclusions, as we have changed two things at once there, which is rarely a good idea). We can't shift thousands of people from a desert climate to the tundra to study what changes, such as whether the murder rate goes up. The best we can manage at present is increasing the probability of rain in a particular location by seeding the clouds by spraying them with small particles, such as of silver iodide, and even this manipulation has limited success. As we can't carry out controlled experiments, we must rely on observational correlational studies, where we look at what people in different climates do differently. With a bit of thought we can be a bit clever, such as looking at hot days in cold climates or cold days in hot climates, but our options are clearly limited.

All these factors make the weather an interesting but difficult topic for studying psychology in the real world empirically because it is so complicated, but also because we have plausible intuitions about how phenomena are related, and for once we have masses of data. It is scientifically challenging to ask: how can we draw sound conclusions with complex setups where many things are going on and changing at the same time? It is fortunate that there is a lot of weather and many, many people upon which the weather is acting because we can anticipate that we are unlikely to find very large effects on behaviour due to meteorological variables, or else these ideas would be enshrined in law, and every time hot weather is forecast there would be a red warning for psychopathic killers at large. It's likely that effects are small, and therefore we will need to be alert to possible confounding variables, and we should always remember that we are at best constructing arguments based on limited data.

The study of psychology and the weather is a microcosm of psychology; as we shall see, all the major debates present in the social sciences are present here.

CLIMATE AND PERSONALITY

Before we go any further we must distinguish between climate and weather. The *climate* of a region is the "average" weather over a long period of time. We can't choose too long a period because climate changes, so the standard measure is the average over 30 years.

The *weather* is what is happening now. We might be living in an area with a hot, dry, sunny desert climate, but today it happens to be snowing heavily. The long-term hot, dry pattern is the climate, and the snowing today aspect is the weather. Weather and climate comprise several variables, including temperature, humidity, wind direction, wind speed, precipitation type, and atmospheric pressure, but these variables are not independent – for example in the northern hemisphere, northerly winds generally correspond to lower temperatures, and southerly winds to higher, and falling pressure is associated with higher precipitation rates. A climate is defined by a pattern of scores on these variables: a desert is dry, a rain forest hot and wet, and a temperate climate doesn't score at the extremes very often on any of the variables. Importantly the dominant type of vegetation varies with climate – you won't find many rainforests growing in a cold, dry tundra. The climate is made up of average weather.

The best-known classification of climates is the *Köppen scheme*, named after the Russian-German weather scientist Vladimir Köppen (1846–1940). He divided climates into five broad groups: tropical, dry, temperate (a big group varying from Mediterranean to Highland), continental, and polar, each broad group having several subdivisions. So northwest Europe is Cfb (temperate without dry season and having a warm summer); the northeast US is Dfa in the south (cold continental without dry season and having a hot summer) and Dfb in the north (cold continental without dry season and having a warm summer); and North Africa is BWh (arid desert and hot).

Surely people who live in sunny, warm climates are happier, more relaxed, and more easy-going than those of us born into a dark, cold climate? Surely mental illness, particularly depression, is less common if the sun is always shining?

The problem with testing this idea is that many things vary systematically with climate. By "systematically" we mean that if we change one thing, something else nearly always changes as well. Let's consider just the weather of particular places: desert climates, for example, are dry, sunny, and hot, but which of those three factors, or combination of them, might affect our behaviour? And then very cold climates are further north (and south, although not many people live in Antarctica), where we observe dramatic variations in the length of daylight – perhaps it isn't the cold that gets to people, but the lack of sunlight in winter, or perhaps it's both?

Even more complex are cultural differences that might vary with the climate. For example, as a very general rule, the nearer the equator you get the hotter it gets, but the greater is the proportion of people living in poverty or extreme poverty. But perhaps the poverty is in part a consequence of the climate; it seems very plausible to me that if it is too hot, people are unable to work as much and as hard, and so productivity and the gross national product decline. And if it's too dry, crops will be more difficult to grow, and so crop failures and famine will be common. Of course money isn't everything, and possibly money comes at the cost of happiness, but starvation is bad no matter how happy you might be.

We believe that there is an optimum climate, with a mean temperature around 22°C, without extreme variation and without too many violent weather events, such as big storms, droughts, and heatwaves. A location can, however, have an average temperature of 22°C, but that average can occur because it is pretty much 22° all the time (very nice, particularly if it's a little cooler at night), or because it's 35° in the summer and beneath freezing for much of the rest of the year (not so nice). Precipitation can come as rain or snow; we can have 1000 mm distributed pretty evenly across the year (nice), or with much of it falling in one or two "monsoon months", and very dry the rest of the time (troubling). So in addition to the average of the meteorological variables, the range and distribution matter too, and together they determine the climate.

A person's personality is those more permanent aspects of the way in which he or she behaves. An extravert tends to be outgoing and sociable, and an introvert less so. There are many ways of measuring human personality, but one of the most robust and most used schemes to have emerged in recent times is the "Big Five" model. When we measure personality, we ask people to take personality tests, which contain many questions where you have to score how you feel on statements such as "I would rather go to a party than stay in reading a book". If you look at how many people respond to personality tests, many minor aspects of personality can be clustered together to form the five independent personality dimensions of *openness* (how open you are to new experiences), *conscientiousness* (self-explanatory), *extraversion* (how outgoing you are), *agreeableness* (how altruistic and kind you are), and *neuroticism* (how anxious and irritable you are). These dimensions helpfully form the acronym OCEAN. Scores on personality variables need not be completely static across a person's lifespan: I am sure I have become slightly more extravert as I have got older; and they may change slightly across situations: a glass of wine makes me more extravert. However, in contrast to a person's mood, personality is relatively stable.

The meteorological variable that has most effect on personality is variation in temperature. Two large-scale studies by Wei and colleagues looked at how people scored on personality tests across many areas of China and the US. They found that the average ambient temperature during someone's youth was related to scores measuring the "Big Five" personality variables. Temperature particularly affected scores on the openness factor, particularly finer-grained measures of socialisation (how well a person internalises society's norms) and personal growth (how open a person is to new experiences). One obvious possibility is that such climate enables developing individuals to explore the external environment, hence influencing their personality development. Essentially it's easy for children to wander around exploring the outside world if it's nice all the time, and less easy if they're snowed in for half the year. Within the US these constraints mean that if all other things are equal (a big if), a child growing up in southern California is likely to be friendlier, more outgoing, and more inquisitive than a child growing up having to deal with the brutal winters of Minnesota (in spite of the many advantages of that beautiful state).

I should reiterate the caveat that this research is correlational, as we can measure only the effects of climate on variables of interest, and it is worth repeating that climate varies with many other factors, such as geographic and regional genetic variations, culture, levels of disease and poverty, and history. Also the differences we find are small, and of course many other things are going on as well. A warm, sunny climate by no means guarantees an outgoing child.

CLIMATE AND INTELLIGENCE

Individual differences include personality, gender differences, and intelligence. Are there other individual differences that vary with climate? It has been known for some time that temperature affects the sex ratio of reptiles through a *thermosensitive period* of egg development; in many species of turtle, eggs in cooler conditions hatch as male, and eggs in warmer as female. Perhaps surprisingly weather and climate may affect the human sex ratio, with a study in Japan showing more girls being born in warmer weather and hotter climates. Other studies suggest that it isn't just warmer weather as such but more extreme weather that increases the ratio of female births, with one possible mechanism being that male foetuses are more susceptible to external stressors, including extreme weather. However, the results across several studies are not totally clear-cut: one study found that more boys were born in spells of warmer weather in northern Finland. One explanation is that the variations have to be relatively extreme to reduce the number of boys, as was the case in Japan, but not in Finland.

At present we are talking about relatively small differences, with the birth ratio varying from about 1.04 boys for every girl to 1.07, but if the climate changes to produce global warming and more extreme weather, the ratio will change more, with more females being born than males, at least until evolution has time to catch up with any changes. We already observe dramatic changes in the ratio of male to female sea turtles in Australia, with up to 99% of births in some areas being female. It's unlikely that boys will disappear altogether, but in some parts of the world male births are already valued more than female births, and this problem could be exacerbated.

Intelligence is conventionally measured by IQ (intelligence quotient) tests. Authors of these tests now proclaim them to be "culture-free" (i.e., they don't ask you questions such as who won the World Series in 2013 and declare you dumb if you don't know). A great deal of research has shown that average IQ varies around the world, both across nations and within them. Many studies have found that both IQ and measures of attainment in school vary with climatic differences between geographical locations such that, essentially, the colder the climate, the higher the IQ of the resident population. Harsh winters are good for the population's intelligence.

The cross-cultural variation in IQ is surprisingly large, with a mean IQ score ranging from 64 in Mozambique to 108 in Hong Kong. We observe effects within countries as well as across them, such as in the United States. Massachusetts, New Hampshire, and Vermont have higher average IQ, and California, Louisiana, and Mississippi have lower scores.

Of course climate is not the only variable likely to have an effect on IQ here, but statistical analyses show that it does make a clear contribution: too hot leads to lower IQ. Why might this be? The theory of cold winters proposes that survival in colder climates poses two evolutionary problems that would have required high intelligence to solve: finding food and keeping warm. Many of the arguments involved are speculative, and the obvious answers are not necessarily right. On finding food, one argument is that hunting in the grasslands of Europe and Asia was more difficult than hunting in the woodlands of Africa because grasslands provide less cover; however, humans evolved in the relatively open savannah, not in dense forests. The peoples of the Arctic endure the harshest winter conditions of all, and by this sort of argument should have a very high IQ, but the average IQ of Arctic people in these studies was rather low, at 91, although it's been noted that Arctic peoples have a very strong visual memory. Another argument, proposed by Satoshi Kanazawa, is that evolution favours high IQ as we go further from the evolutionary origin of humans in sub-Saharan Africa; staying put is the lazy option, while exploring new environments is more intellectually taxing.

None of these arguments is that convincing, and they all leave a slightly unpleasant taste in the mouth because there is no certainty that the studies adequately take into account the obvious reasons for cross-cultural variation in IQ scores: differences in the culture's attitude and experience with the tests, education, poverty, colonialism, nutrition, and disease. The argument that factors such as geography and climate are important because you find effects within a country such as the United States is fallacious because different areas of the US show wide variations in income, education, and disease. Few things drive psychologists into a frenzy as much as the suggestion that there are possible differences in any kind of aptitude relating to race.

Some recent studies have found that levels of infectious disease affect IQ, controlling for the effects of education, national wealth, temperature, and distance from sub-Saharan Africa; in particular parasite load is particularly important: children with heavy intestinal worm infestations tend to have lower IQs. Parasite loads affect the strength of the immune system, in that if the body is expending so much energy fighting off parasite infections, other systems are likely to be compromised. (There is some evidence though that very low parasite loads might be good for the immune system, perhaps we are now in the west too clean.)

There are some less controversial differences in cognitive skills that vary with climate. Many languages of the world (English is not one) use tone, or pitch, to give meaning to their words. The American linguist Caleb Everett and his collaborators have found that languages with complex tones, those that use several pitches for making contrasts in meaning, are much more likely to occur in humid regions of the world, while languages where pitch doesn't make much difference to meaning occur more frequently in drier regions. The favoured explanation is that inhaling dry air causes the larynx to become dehydrated and reduces the elasticity of the vocal chords. So it's physically more difficult to achieve complex tones in dry climates, especially cold ones.

SEASON OF BIRTH AND PERSONALITY

A climate is not uniform throughout the year; there can be some dramatic changes from month to month. We call these annual variations in climate seasons. In the northern hemisphere, north of the tropics, there is a winter season that is colder than the summer season. There is some evidence that your later personality is affected by when you were born: the season of your birth has been shown to be associated with both later personality type and susceptibility to different types of mental illness.

There are several differences in personality dependent on the season of your birth. The results are a bit messy, and the effects are small, and not all studies have found them, but in general, people born in summer tend to be slightly healthier and slightly more outgoing. People born in summer are also more likely than those born in winter to have a *cyclothymic* personality, which is characterised by frequent mood swings, between happy and sad. Those born in the winter have a higher chance of being less irritable. People born in spring and summer are more likely to have lower anxiety-related traits and higher approach-related traits (e.g., novelty seeking) than those born in winter. Children born between March and July tend to be shyer.

Some of these effects may be moderated by gender. A study in Japan found seasonal variations in some personality traits, such as being self-directed and the likelihood of persevering with tasks, but only in females. The researchers found that the most important variable in their study was ambient temperature, although the method illustrates the difficulty of carrying out this type of research: how fine-grained should the analysis be? In this study researchers had access only to the average temperature for the month of birth, and the temperature for Tokyo rather than the actual birth area. Suppose, though, that the child is born in a very hot but short heatwave in an otherwise very cool summer month. There is also an interaction between gender and season of birth with regards to conscientiousness, with males showing greater variation in scores. Another complication is that circadian preference may temper the way season of birth affects personality traits. Some of us are "morning types", waking up bright and breezy and ready to get straight on with things, but flagging as the day progresses, while others are "evening types", acting the other way round. People born during autumn and winter show a more marked morning preference compared to those born during spring and summer. Evening types tend to score lower on conscientiousness than morning types, so it is difficult to tease apart what is causal here. Our circadian preferences change during our lives: morning preference is more frequent than evening preference until adolescence and also after 50 years, with adolescence associated with a shift from morning to evening types. These observations might explain why we find different season of birth effects on personality in adolescents and young adults compared to adults.

There are many possible reasons for these effects, including the likelihood of infection, seasonal changes in diet and nutrition, external toxins, weather influence, such as humidity or temperature, type of recreational habit, the ability of the parent to exercise, and the way in which physical development and psychological development are affected by sunlight. There could be effects on the pregnant mother, the newborn infant, or both.

Another possibility is that the *brain-derived neurotrophic factor* gene (BDNF) is involved in personality traits. This gene controls the expression of BDNF, a special protein called a *neurotrophin* that affects the growth of nerve cells. The production of BDNF is sensitive to many factors, including the amount of exercise and the diet, all of which could be plausibly affected by the season. Diet tends to be better in spring and summer, with higher levels of iron, zinc, and vitamin B. Dietary differences might be more pronounced in poorer societies, but people like me hardly live in poverty, and I tend to have more and varied fruit and vegetables in summer.

Seasonal factors may also influence the distribution of genes by influencing conception, either through the probability of the survival of a foetus or an infant, or through the conception practices of the parents. Certain genes associated with emotional regulation are slightly more likely to be active in children born in summer, and less active in children born in autumn. This genetic effect might be one way in which season of birth affects the level of neurotransmitters.

Babies are more likely to be born at some times of year, and that time of year turns out perhaps surprisingly to depend upon where your mother lives. Throughout the northern hemisphere the north exhibits peak birth rates in spring and summer, and, while the further south you go the more births tend to peak later in the year, the further south you go the more pronounced these differences also are, at least in the United States. The birth peak occurs in November in Florida, but June in Ohio. What's more, recently the peaks have tended to occur later in the year. These effects are observed within a single large country, such as the United States, suggesting that they are not caused wholly by variations in factors such as gross national product or ethnicity. Needless to say there are exceptions, such as Italy in the 1970s and early 1980s, which had a birth peak in March.

In terms of conception, these findings mean that in more northerly latitudes people tend to conceive more in autumn, but those further south are doing so more in winter. Now this result is certainly at odds with the spring fling, the idea that as the sap rises so does a young man's fancy. But it takes two to tango; perhaps the woman is aiming to give birth at a more auspicious time? There is some evidence (from condom manufacturers of all people) that Americans at least are more likely to do it – or at least buy condoms, which probably has a complex relationship with conception data – when it's hot, which is at odds with the birthdate data. There's a secondary peak in condom sales in December, perhaps influenced by the Christmas party season, and a peak in termination of pregnancies a few weeks later. There are other factors in addition to sexual practices, because sperm concentration and motility vary across the year, peaking in summer. Dairy cows inseminated in high summer are less fertile than those inseminated when it is less hot. We face the complicated picture that people are most likely to do it when they are less fertile. Early infant mortality and early childhood diseases might also play a major role in birthday variation.

Finally environmental conditions may well influence the course of pregnancy. There is evidence that both birthweight and body-mass index are lower in people, especially females, born in months with higher ambient temperature. This relationship may arise because of the effect of ambient temperature on blood flow though the placenta at a period of rapid foetal development. It is also known that later BMI is associated with some personality measures. For example, heavier-weight females tend to have lower levels of self-esteem than lower-weight females, and self-esteem is in turn associated with self-directedness – the ability to take control of your life and make decisions. This association is less pronounced in males. Such mechanisms clearly account for some of the relationships found, as well as indicating how they might be moderated by variables such as gender.

So the season of our birth affects our personality in small but notable ways. It's difficult to give any simple summary because factors such as gender and morningness-eveningness affect personality development and also vary with season of birth.

HOW WEATHER INFLUENCES MOOD

I am sitting with my computer writing this section at midday on a cold, grey January's day. At this time of year the sun is supposed to rise at 8:45 a.m., but in fact climbs over the hill at 9:30, and is supposed to set at 3:45 p.m., but again in practice sinks behind another hill at around 2:30 (yes, really) – although on a day like today all talk of "the sun" is academic, as there is thick cloud and a layer of murk beneath it, transforming the land into eternal twilight. Grey is the colour most associated with anxiety and depression (it's yellow for feeling good). It is very difficult for me to imagine that the weather isn't contributing to my strong sense of gloom.

Three things are going on here. First, there's the climate: Scotland is usually cool in winter (never hot), and often cloudy and wet. Second, there's the effect of latitude: Scotland is quite far north, which means it has long summer days but long winter nights. Third, there's the weather: today is particularly miserable, but there are some glorious sunny but cold days where the cold doesn't seem to matter because the sun is shining and the sky is a wonderful blue colour. Although weather and climate are of course related, we will look at the effects of both on mood.

What is mood, though? Mood is a temporary state distinguished from a person's personality. Measures of personality variables are relatively stable across time; no one wakes up a closed introvert one day and a brazen extravert the next, although of course people do change gradually. Personality is moderated by mood – an underlying extravert can one day feel rather quiet, subdued, and a bit down; and personality and mood are related – someone scoring highly on neuroticism is more likely to feel anxious at any particular time. The most basic division of mood is into positive and negative affect – good and bad mood. The simplest and most obvious hypothesis is that good climates predispose people to better average mood. What could be more plausible than the suggestion that when the sun shines and the mercury rises, we feel good, but when it is dull and damp, we feel miserable?

It turns out that it is difficult to find robust evidence for simple effects of weather on mood and cognition. The largest recent study was carried out by Jaap Denissen and his colleagues in Berlin in 2008. This study was important because it used a very large sample of participants (over 1,200) linked to local weather station data and used a sophisticated statistical analysis. The effects of weather on mood were quite complex but most importantly very small. Perhaps on reflection we shouldn't be too surprised by the effects being small; at any one time the weather is just one of many things affecting what we do, and often a rather peripheral thing – and of course these days we live much of our lives indoors. The effects of variables such as amount of sunshine are indeed stronger among people who spend more time outside. What's more, there is a large variation between individuals, which again on reflection is perhaps not surprising. Some people are particularly sensitive to the duration of day, which in retrospect we might expect given how some but not all people might suffer from a seasonal affective disorder.

What then are the factors that affect us? The study looked at the effects of the weather on affect – mood – and levels of tiredness. Participants kept a diary tracking these variables. The results showed that the principal meteorological variables that affect us are the temperature, wind, and amount of sunlight. Low mood was related to temperature, the amount of sunshine, and the strength of the wind; tiredness was related to sunshine. There were also effects of whether it was raining and of atmospheric pressure, but the sophisticated statistical analysis showed that these were primarily due to the amount of sunshine (it's not sunny when it's raining and tends to be sunny when pressure is high). Several other studies have found broadly consistent results, and it should be said that in line with the small effect sizes some studies failed to find any relationship at all. Similar effects are found on cognitive skills; digit span, a measure of memory, increases on nice sunny days when the pressure is climbing, particularly among people who work outdoors.

The variables which appear to have the greatest effect on mood are humidity, temperature, and the hours of sunshine, but again their effects are rather specific and not always predictable. As we might expect, high levels of humidity lower scores on measures of concentration and cause an increase in sleepiness. Less predictable is the finding that rising temperatures lower anxiety and make people less sceptical, of all things.

Other studies have shown that good weather broadens the mind, broadening cognitive style – we become more open-minded and inclined to take on board new information; we might even become more creative. As the sun shines, we become more optimistic: the number of hours of sunshine predicts score on ratings of optimism.

The overall conclusion is that there are effects of weather on mood and cognition, but they're weak and variable. It isn't just cognitive effects; a recent study has shown that wet weather doesn't affect joint pain. One aspect of the perhaps surprising difficulty in finding weather effects on mood and cognition I find mysterious is that we know humans are susceptible to influence and bias, an example being the placebo effect, whereby just having treatment, such as a little white sugar pill, can be beneficial. So if we believe that sunshine makes us happier, why doesn't it do so more obviously, even the absence of other biological mechanisms? One possibility is that it would actually be maladaptive for stimuli such as the weather to have too great an effect; after all, if hunter-gatherers stopped hunting because it was a nice sunny day, there would be trouble. We also adapt to pleasant stimuli, so after a while they stop having such a large effect. There is evidence for this idea in that sunny warm days have more of a beneficial effect in spring, when they start occurring again after their absence in winter.

Many studies don't look at how long people spend outside – perhaps we don't find any effect of weather on mood because these days we're all stuck in windowless offices and have no idea what is going on outside. Studies do support this idea, to some extent; another study by Keller and colleagues looked at this variable and found that people who spend more time outdoors do have their moods lifted by good weather. But in keeping with all the other studies the effects were still very small overall.

Another important variable is individual differences in preference for certain types of weather, in that different people often like different sorts of weather: some like it hot, but not everyone does. Indeed the same person may think different things at different times; for example, I usually love a heavy snowfall, and even enjoy the possibility of being snowed in, but if I have an important trip to make my attitude is very different. An important study by Klimstra and colleagues found that people can be broadly divided into "Summer Lovers" and "Summer Haters". Summer Lovers enjoy a warm and sunny day, while Summer Haters have relatively better moods on a cool and cloudy day. More generally there are three main types of people: some like sunshine and warmth, others don't like it too hot, and some just don't like rain. There is some evidence that these likes and dislikes run in the family, which on reflection is not that surprising.

We also need to explain why so many people believe so strongly that weather affects them when often it doesn't. One explanation is that the idea is culturally transmitted – we believe it because so many other people do. We could also be disproportionately influenced by hearing about people with seasonal affective disorder.

Nevertheless it is curious that there is no strong placebo effect. We know from studies in many different areas that people just have to believe something works for it to work, such as taking a sugar pill when being told by a doctor that it will stop their headache for it to indeed stop that headache, even though it has absolutely no active ingredients. So if we believe so strongly that the weather affects our moods, why don't all studies clearly demonstrate this effect of belief? It is all rather mysterious.

2

WEATHER AND HEALTH

SEASONAL AFFECTIVE DISORDER

The study of the relationship between weather and health is called *biometeorology*. While some effects are on reflection very plausible, others are rather more surprising, and the underlying mechanics of the link are sometimes poorly understood. In extreme cases lack of sunshine can lead to clinical depression, a disorder known as *seasonal affective disorder* (SAD). SAD is marked by symptoms of clinical depression occurring in late autumn and winter, and normal or even slightly elevated mood (known as *hypomania*) in spring and summer. SAD sufferers may also show extreme fatigue, extra sleepiness and difficulty waking, and weight gain in winter, symptoms not typically associated with non-seasonal depression. Low mood can be accompanied by several other characteristics, such as an increased need for sleep, carbohydrate craving, and a noticeable decrement in cognitive performance. It's estimated that 5% of Americans may suffer from SAD; SAD is four times more in common in women than men, particularly in women of child-bearing age, and people typically start suffering in early adulthood, although children can be affected.

Naturally sunshine is more likely to be lacking in winter, when because of the tilt of the earth on its axis days are shorter in the northern hemisphere, and get shorter the further north you go. Daylight

is at its shortest on the winter solstice, which in the northern hemisphere is around 21 December. In Casablanca on that day sunrise is
at 7:30 and sunset is at 17:26; in London the figures are 8:03 and
15:53; in my hometown of Dundee it is 8:44 and 15:35; but in somewhere like Tromsø, Norway, which is north of the Arctic Circle, there
is no daylight at all (and in fact there isn't any between 28 November
and 15 January). In northern latitudes even if there is sun in principle
it might be greatly reduced by hills.

The body has natural rhythms that get entrained to the external
cycle of light and dark, called circadian rhythms. The rhythms are
governed by the absence of and exposure to bright light falling on the
eye. A part of the brain called the *suprachiasmatic nuclei* (SCN), located at
the front part of the hypothalamus quite near the centre of the brain,
plays an important role as a biological clock. It governs the timing
of the switching on of the pineal gland, a pea-shaped gland hanging
from the brain that produces the hormone *melatonin*. The increase of
melatonin in the blood throughout the day is correlated with fading
light and particularly decreasing blue light, and also with our feeling less alert and more tired. There are a number of receptor sites for
melatonin in the brain, including the SCN, but the exact way in which
melatonin makes us feel tired and helps us to fall asleep is not known.
One study showed that levels of the neurotransmitter serotonin, a
chemical in the brain that acts as a messenger for the system that
regulates mood, rise and fall in line with levels of naturally occurring
sunlight, so presumably melatonin governs the levels of serotonin in
some way. It is worth noting that low levels serotonin are thought to
be implicated in mood disorders, which is how drugs such as fluox-
etine and citalopram may have their effect. Melatonin doesn't directly
cause sleep, even though some take it as a sleep aid, but it does seem
to signal that it's dark and therefore that we should sleep.

A few psychiatrists dispute the existence of SAD as a separate disorder, saying instead it reflects the "pathologisation" of everyday life, in
that we take normal behaviours (whatever that means) and call them
abnormal, and the multiplication of psychiatric disorders, where we
incline towards everything a label. Nevertheless the symptomatology

of SAD is distinct from clinical depression, and the quality of depression often severe enough to merit a psychiatric label. It is recognised in the APA's *Diagnostic and Statistical Manual of Mental Disorders, Fifth Edition* (DSM-5), the official classification of mental disorders, as a qualifier of depression, as "with seasonal pattern", for recurrent major depressive disorder.

If you think you suffer from SAD you have several options. Naturally, severe depression needs medical treatment. You could head south to somewhere warm and sunny; I recommend southern California, and I have a friend who overwinters in Australia. If you're looking for something cheaper and closer to home you should consider getting hold of a SAD light, which provides you with bright white and blue light. Most indoor light bulbs aren't bright enough and emit too little at the higher frequencies, so you need a special bulb that emits more blue light, thereby mimicking sunshine, and that is very bright – at least 10,000 lux – the lux being the SI (the International System of Units) unit of luminance, being equal to one lumen per square metre. The lumen is the derived SI unit of luminous flux. Or if you prefer, the more lux, the brighter it seems, and 10,000 lux is very bright – if you're standing by a window on a bright spring day, but not looking directly at the sun, you're getting about 2500 lux, and most household bulbs emit less than 300 lux. Many bulbs sold as "natural daylight" emit more blue light, and might be more pleasant to look at, but are not bright enough. The theory is of course that the SAD light replaces natural daylight. SAD lights appear to have beneficial effects among non-clinically depressed people too, and the effects occur quickly with just a short exposure to a bright white light.

Another thing sufferers can do is to spend more time outdoors. In and experiment in the United States, participants who spent more time outdoors on warm, sunny, high-pressure days showed improved mood and cognitive skills. It should be pointed out, though, that this experiment was conducted in late spring and summer; it is unclear whether there would be similar benefits in winter, when the sun is much weaker (and UVB light very weak, and hence vitamin D production much less or non-existent in the north). Exercising outdoors in as bright a light as possible (which in winter usually means choosing your time of day, or even your day) is particularly effective.

Animals, including humans, evolved to sleep when it's dark, and artificial light is a very recent evolutionary event. There is much evidence that night-time light is a very bad thing, leading to sleep disruption and mood disorders, reducing our ability to concentrate, interfering with hormone function and food metabolism, weakening the immune system, increasing the stress response, and increasing the chance of some cancers, particularly breast cancer. Light is our natural cue for entraining us to the day-night cycle, and artificial light disrupts and desynchronises our natural circadian rhythms. The mechanisms of this disruption are complex. Exposure to artificial light, particularly blue light, reduces the production of melatonin, a hormone produced by the pineal gland attached to the brain that plays an important role in regulating our sleep-wakefulness cycle.

It is probably impractical to require us all to try to go to sleep as soon as it gets dark, particularly in a northern winter, but we can avoid too much bright blue-white light in the evening. SAD lights should be used in the morning. Even when it's dark it's not usually really dark for most of us, as light pollution hides the stars and electric lights outside our bedrooms illuminate our rooms even when we eventually switch out lights off.

Can you have too much of a good thing? North of the Arctic there are times around the summer solstice on 21 June when the sun never sets; at good old Tromsø the sun never sets between 19 May and 26 July. Obviously being in the sun too long can give you sunburn, but what about the simple effects of light? There is an episode of the old surreal comedy *Northern Exposure*, set in Alaska, where in midsummer everyone goes slightly mad in an interesting and cute sort of way. Some people are sensitive to light at night and in the absence of thick curtains find it difficult to sleep, so we can expect some effects of sleep deprivation in summer in northern latitudes. Sufferers from the disorder known as reverse seasonal affective disorder fare very well in winter but become depressed and anxious, having trouble sleeping, and lose weight in summer, possibly because sensitivity to too much sunlight affects melatonin production, because sleep patterns are affected by staying up too late and not having sufficient darkness, or because high temperatures affect the thyroid and hormone regulation. Reverse SAD is less well known and less understood than SAD, and may be under-diagnosed. At the moment it's estimated that a tenth of all SAD cases are reverse SAD. The treatment is the reverse of that for SAD: maximise time in the dark, or at least away from sunshine, later in the day. American sufferers are advised to turn up the air conditioning.

SEASON OF BIRTH AND MENTAL ILLNESS

We've seen that the season of birth affects a person's personality, so it wouldn't be surprising if it also affects people's predisposition towards suffering from mental illness. Late summer and autumn babies are less likely to suffer from depression than winter babies. There is an excess in babies born through winter to June of major depression, bipolar disorder, eating disorders, autism, and developmental disorders. Perhaps paradoxically, people born in spring and early summer who do suffer from depression tend to first show major symptoms at an early age, and show a more severe clinical course. So you are less likely to suffer from severe depression if you're born in late spring or early summer, but if you do suffer it will start earlier and be worse.

Following on from this pattern of severe major depression being linked with spring and summer births, there is an elevated risk of successful suicide among people born in spring and summer. The biggest increase (7.6%) in suicide risk is among people born in July. The associations between season of birth and the risk of completed suicide are stronger among males and among those who committed suicide using violent methods (e.g., by using firearms, throwing oneself off a building or in front of a train, or hanging) than among those who chose non-violent methods (e.g., a drug overdose). It could be that those using a violent method are more determined that the suicide attempt will be successful.

On the other hand, there is a significant excess of babies born from August to November in patients with clinical OCD (obsessive-compulsive disorder), and a significant decrease of births from March to July.

One of the best-known seasonal variations is in schizophrenia, a severe mental illness, or psychosis, marked by delusions, thought disorder, and hallucinations, particularly auditory hallucinations (voices in the head). In the northern hemisphere people are more likely to develop schizophrenia if they're born in winter or early spring, particularly February and March, and less likely if they are born from late spring to autumn, particularly July to October. The differences, while not huge, are notable, with an increase of up to 10% for those winter months.

It is likely that several factors are operating, particularly given that different disorders peak at different times of year. I remember from my undergraduate days a long time ago that the schizophrenia winter peak was well known, and the dominant idea then was that it was mostly due to an as yet unidentified virus affecting the mother. This idea hasn't had any traction. The most popular theory is that lack of sunshine and vitamin D deficiency are involved, and if that is so, the problem is solved simply by taking more milk or even just vitamin D supplementation. The exact mechanism by which vitamin D deficiency causes schizophrenia is not clear, but there is most likely some relationship between the deficiency, the immune system, and inflammation. Vitamin D reduces the levels of cytokines, which are small but important proteins that are now known to play an important role in signalling in the immune system. Vitamin D also plays a part in the way genes are expressed. Finally, low levels of vitamin D during pregnancy affect the brain structures that are involved in schizophrenia, particularly the systems involved with the neurotransmitter dopamine. The importance of vitamin D isn't confined to the time of birth, because childhood deficiency also leads to a worse prognosis.

Given the pervasive and strong effects of vitamin D on physical and mental health, and given that vitamin D production is clearly linked to the amount of sunshine, it is likely that sunshine levels during pregnancy and childhood and adolescence, at least, affect brain development and brain states in ways we have not yet uncovered.

WEATHER AND SUICIDE

If weather and climate affect mood, you might expect the suicide rate to increase markedly in the depths of winter. What could be more miserable than a cold, wet, dark midwinter's day? Surely that's when people who are already very depressed and feeling suicidal are most likely to be pushed over the edge and kill themselves? Surely as well the further north you go in winter, the longer the period of darkness, and so the higher the suicide rate should be? That's the common belief, yet here folk psychology is wrong. To many people's surprise, the prevalence of suicide is in fact higher in late spring and early summer.

People's incorrect beliefs are not helped by the press, who on this topic often get it wrong and go with lay beliefs rather than data: in December 2000 the Annenberg Public Policy Center in Los Angeles published findings of its analysis of suicides during the 1999 winter holidays to 100 newspapers across the United States. The press release highlighted the fact that the majority of the 64 stories linking suicide with the holiday season from 8 November 1999 (as everywhere, the winter holiday season starts early in LA) up to 15 January 2000. The press summaries either implied or directly attributed the cause of suicide to the holiday season. But of course the press articles didn't tell us how many people killed themselves in a similar period a few months later; without an appropriate comparison, we cannot draw any conclusions.

It should be said, though, that these effects are relatively weak, vary from place to place, and might be moderated by gender. Estimates suggest that suicide is very slightly more common in summer (26%, against an expected 25% for one of the four seasons) and lowest in winter (24%), but effects of days of the week are stronger (with slightly more suicides occurring on Wednesday and slightly fewer on Thursday). The suicide peak is later in the year for women. Seasonality in suicide is more pronounced the more agricultural a society is – people working in agriculture are much more likely to be working outside. The industrialisation of western society has seen a great shift away from working on the land, which may explain why these seasonal effects are becoming weaker. The seasonal peak is stronger for violent suicides (e.g., shooting yourself, hanging, or jumping from a high roof) than non-violent (e.g., using drugs, or gas). Male farmers are particularly prone to suicide (there were nearly 1,000 between 1982 and 1999 in England and Wales); there are probably several factors at work here, including relatively easy access to means, such as shotguns, but it is entirely possible that spending a great deal of time outdoors strengthens the seasonal drive. Rural areas generally across the world experience slightly higher suicide rates than urban areas.

Why is the peak much later than the worst weather, when things are getting better? Researchers have proposed several explanations, and there might be something in all of them.

It is widely believed that revolutions happen only when things are starting to get better, or when things are getting better but not quickly enough. Although I have been unable to find any data to support this belief, with a little thought the belief sounds plausible because when people are too impoverished and disempowered and the agents of the state sufficiently strong, a successful revolt stands little chance of success – history is littered with examples of quickly crushed revolts and surprisingly long-lasting oppressive regimes. Perhaps the same principle applies with oppressive weather: when it is dark all the time maybe we are too depressed to act, and it is only when things improve a little that we have the energy or ability to kill ourselves. The French sociologist Emile Durkheim (1858–1917), in his famous 1897 monograph *Suicide*, noted that there was a suicide peak in late spring, and proposed a variant of this explanation, saying that in spring we note that everything is starting to wake up, other people are starting to rouse from their slumbers and cheer up, and the number of pleasant social interactions among other people increases. In other words, the comparison between a depressed and non-depressed person is more striking; in winter everyone is a bit down, but when spring comes we, the depressed people, are suddenly noticeably relatively worse off.

Other explanations of the spring suicide peak include seasonal hormonal changes. There are seasonal fluctuations in hormone levels in women, which might explain the moderating effect of gender: oestrogen and progesterone affect circadian rhythms, again in a complex way which presently isn't well understood.

If dull weather and lack of sunshine are a factor in suicide, then we should also expect the suicide rate in winter to increase the further north we go. While this expectation is very broadly true there are a large number of qualifications. First, we are handicapped by a lack of reliable data from many parts of the world, particularly Africa and large parts of Asia. Second, the recording of suicide might not be wholly reliable; there is a widespread taboo against suicide, and many countries might be reluctant to record the real numbers. Third, while the pattern is true in the northern hemisphere, it does not appear to be so in the south (where if course the winter weather occurs in the northern summer months); however, the population density is much lower in the south, and very few people live very far south. As ever there is a large possible confound between latitude and other factors, such as poverty; the nearer the equator you get, the more poverty increases. It is entirely possible that poverty in poor countries protects against suicide; or that suicide has a cultural aspect so that, without wishing in any way to diminish the misery and suffering that lead to suicide, you have to have a certain minimal level of subsistence for it to be a possibility.

If we consider the extremes across the world, the countries of Eastern Europe and East Asia have the highest suicide rate in the world. The region with the lowest suicide rate is Latin America. Russia has extreme winters and vast expanses of land close to or above the Arctic circle. The World Health Organisation (WHO) figures for 2015 give a suicide rate of 179 per million in Russia. One possible confounding factor is the high level of alcoholism in Russia, the post-Soviet states, and Eastern Europe, which have the highest levels in the world. But although the rate is high, Russia is only seventeenth in the rate of suicide in 2015; Sri Lanka and Guyana top the list, with more than 300 suicides per million.

You might also expect the suicide rate to be high in Scandinavia, which at a high latitude sees long, dark, cold winters. The rates in Scandinavia are indeed generally higher than the average for Europe (142 per million for Finland and 127 for Sweden, compared with an average for Europe of 119), but in Norway, which has some of the furthest north territory in the world, it is only 93.

In addition to these geographical variations, the figures change with time. In 2009 Lithuania had the highest suicide rate among the countries for which we have data, with 286 suicide deaths per million people, followed closely by South Korea, with 263 deaths per million; its unenviable position was taken in 2015 by Sri Lanka. The UK's rate is quite low (60 per million).

Given the many things that differ among countries, it makes sense to take one large country and examine how suicide rates are affected by latitude and climate there, because within a single country many of the factors that vary among countries will remain constant. The United States is a perfect case study because it is generally very affluent and we have fairly reliable data for it. Looking at a map of suicide rate by state, it looks as though there's no simple effect of latitude: the northeast states have lower suicide rates than southern states. The highest rates are found in a swathe of states in the west, particularly New Mexico, Nevada, Wyoming, and Montana, with high rates in surrounding states. There clearly is no major effect of latitude. These states do experience climatic extremes, including desert conditions, high summer temperatures, and extreme variations in temperature over the seasons. Given that the suicide rate is also high in Russia and Asia, we might tentatively conclude that continental climates are associated with a higher rate.

We see, then, that time of year and geography affect suicide rates. What about the weather on a particular day? Is it possible that, in some cases, weather can be the tipping point and lead to a small increase in the suicide rate on dull, wet days? With my colleague Fhionna Moore and others, I examined the effect of weather on suicide rates in Scotland. We found that the amount of rainfall was positively related to both male and female call rates. That is, during times of heavier rain, men and women used the National Health Service "Breathing Space" phone helpline more heavily. Similarly, warmer temperatures and greater hours of sunshine were associated with fewer calls concerning loneliness and self-harm. It is possible that weather conditions impact the likelihood of potential callers being inside, increasing isolation and opportunity for self-harm. Gender difference plays a significant role. Among all age groups in most of the world, females tend to show higher rates of reported non-fatal suicide attempts, while males have a higher rate of completed suicide.

Clearly the pattern is complicated, and climate is just one factor in a panoply of reasons why people take their own lives. All the factors I've discussed have perhaps a surprisingly small effect on suicide rates. People don't kill themselves just because it's a gloomy day in the depths of winter; they can kill themselves at any time, for many reasons. It could be that in some cases the weather or climate can be one of the contributing factors that cause a person to take his or her life just then.

THUNDERSTORMS AND BEHAVIOUR

All my elderly relatives claimed to be able to sense when a thunderstorm was coming on, and were often overjoyed to be proved right, refusing to accept that the soaring temperatures, the falling barometer, and high humidity might have had anything to do with their belief (let alone having heard the weather forecast). There is a widespread belief that humans and animals can sense thunderstorms, and that they can affect our behaviour – and all is well again when the storms and the associated front pass. Anecdotal evidence suggests that children are more restless before thunderstorms, and teaching younger children in class is more difficult.

Perhaps surprisingly, some people are sensitive to exposure to ions. Ions are electrically charged particles, atoms, or molecules formed when they gain or lose electrons. The atmosphere is made up of 78% nitrogen and 21% oxygen, with the rest made up of trace gases, such as carbon dioxide and some water vapour. Nitrogen and oxygen exist mostly as molecules – both with two atoms in each molecule, N_2 and O_2. Normally a nitrogen molecule will contain 14 electrons and an oxygen molecule 16; occasionally through a process called *ionisation* an atom loses an electron leaving the atom with an overall positive charge. Ionisation has many causes: most ions are formed by the small amounts of radioactive elements in the ground or air, some by strikes by cosmic rays, and some by sources of heat, such as lightning strikes.

At sea level the number of ions is small, usually under 1,000 in a cubic centimetre (bearing in mind that at sea level there are around 2.5×10^{25} – that's 25 with 24 zeros after it – atoms in a cubic centimetre), but as we go up in the atmosphere the number increases; in the *ionosphere*, between about 40 and 400 miles, the atmosphere is very strongly ionised because of the stronger effects of solar radiation. Talking of sea level, splashing water causes ionisation (through evaporation), so the concentration of ions can be greater near the sea where waves break on the shore and around waterfalls; the frequently mentioned ozone is not an ion, but an oxygen molecule with three atoms, O_3, and you can't smell ions or ozone – that distinctive odour at the seaside is rotting seaweed. Traffic and power lines generate small numbers of ions locally, and they accumulate indoors with the effects of air conditioning, dust, pollution, electrical equipment, and lack of ventilation.

The production of ions requires an energy source, and lightning is one of the most dramatic natural energy sources there is, so it is not surprising that a large number of ions is generated during a thunderstorm. More curiously, the number of ions in the atmosphere increases several hours before the storm starts. In particular we observe an increase in the number of positive ions, up to 5,000 per cubic centimetre at sea level, as a consequence of lighter negative ions being carried up through the atmosphere in strong convective currents that lead to the development of storms. During the storm the number of positive ions drops back to 500, while the number of negative ions increases to several thousand (depending on the number of lightning strikes).

Research shows that people are sensitive to the concentration and type (positive and negative) of ions. As well as just before storms, positive ions increase with the onset of strong regional winds, such as the Santa Ana in California, the Chinook in the Pacific Northwest, and the Sirocco in Italy. When the concentration of positive ions increases, bad things start happening: the number of car accidents increases, there's more crime, and the suicide rate increases. Individually most people feel more irritable, tense, and depressed, although as ever there is considerable individual variation. Positive ions also tend to increase blood pressure. Positive ions also affect cognitive processing, slowing reaction times. In more extreme cases the ions may trigger headaches, including migraines, and interfere with sleep. Positive ions seem to affect the level of serotonin in the brain; serotonin is a neurotransmitter, a chemical messenger in the brain, particularly involved in regulating mood and aggression – many modern antidepressants have the effect of preventing the reuptake of serotonin in the brain, thereby increasing its availability. Positive ions increase the levels of serotonin dramatically. You can have too much of a good thing, with excess serotonin causing *serotonin syndrome*. Serotonin syndrome can be extremely serious, and can prove fatal, but less extreme cases display headache, stomach upset, increased temperature, and agitation. While antidepressants can take weeks to work, serotonin syndrome can start within minutes of an increase in levels. In a classic series of studies in the early 1970s Felix Sulman, an Israeli pharmacologist, took urine samples from people exposed in the laboratory to an excess of positive ions or an excess of negative ions. As we would expect, positive was bad and negative good. He also looked at people during the Bora and Sharav winds and found a similar pattern of results. The Bora is a very cold wind blowing from the northeast into the Adriatic Sea; the Sharav, or Khamsin, is a very dry, hot, sandy wind blowing from the south in the Arabian Peninsula and North Africa.

Germany sometimes advertises a medication's ability to treat *Föhnkrankheit* or Föhn sickness. Föhn winds roll down mountainsides, warming the weather by up to 28°C in a matter of hours, and they're largely responsible for Central Europe's relatively mild temperatures. Föhn sickness leads to a higher incidence of accidents: researchers found that accident rates at a heavy-machinery plant were especially high, and workers at a second industrial plant were more likely to report to the plant's doctor's office for medical attention during the Föhn. After observing the behaviour of almost 30,000 German exhibition visitors and industrial workers, researchers concluded that Föhn sickness is real. One possibility is that it is caused by mental slowing and lapses of concentration: in one study people were slower to react to visual cues at a traffic exhibition in Munich.

Putting together the findings that the number of ions increases hours before a storm starts and the sensitivity of some people to ion density, it is entirely plausible that some people are sensitive to forthcoming thunderstorms: they detect the increased number of positive ions.

If positive ions have all these negative effects, do negative ions have positive effects? Yes, they do improve mood and cognition, which is one reason why so many might feel better after the storm has passed, although its passing will also be marked by lower humidity and temperature.

It should be stressed that not all studies have found effects of ionisation on health and behaviour. A recent meta-analysis, a technique which pools all the experiments carried out on a particular question and derives a statistic showing whether overall they produce significant effects, failed to find any negative effect of positive ions or positive effect of negative ions on breathing problems, such as asthma and emphysema. Some studies have found effects, but many others haven't, and the effects are weak and sometimes even contradictory. Early experiments in particular tend to suffer from a variety of methodological problems. Sometimes the experiments do not use the important technique of blinding, so that the experimenters or even participants may know which condition they're in. Given the prevalence of the placebo effect, the absence of blinding might be critical when we observe only small effects. Significant experiments haven't revealed *dose-response relationships*, where an increase in the dose of something should produce a bigger effect. Another meta-analysis found no effect of ion levels on anxiety, mood, relaxation, sleep, and personal comfort, but did find that negative air ionisation is associated with lower depression scores, particularly when the levels are very high. There is a suggestion that ion levels play a role in seasonal depression.

Another issue is that although the number of ions sounds large, the concentrations are actually very small. Even 100,000 ions represent an infinitesimally small concentration in the air ($100,000/10^{19}$ molecules in 1 cm³), a concentration smaller than the levels of the presence of the botulism toxin, the most toxic substance widely known to cause illness, so we would have to be extraordinarily sensitive to the effects of positive and negative ions.

There is another caveat: so far we have focused on the positive benefits of negative ions. It is possible that negative ions have unexplored negative effects.

You can buy negative ion generators, which are often combined with air filters. They're fairly cheap and inconspicuous; I have one beside my bed in the hope it will improve my hay fever and help me to wake at 7 a.m. every day, in a Scottish winter, alert and full of energy. Given that negative ions have beneficial effects they should work if they emit enough negative ions to make a difference. There is some tentative experimental evidence that negative ion generators improve the health of office workers. However, these generators also reduce the amount of dust, particulates, and allergens in the air, and it is quite possible that only this function has a beneficial effect.

Finally thunderstorms are formed by strong convective currents in the atmosphere, where hot air at ground level rises, and its place is taken by cold air brought down from higher in the atmosphere, leading to strong down drafts. These down drafts could disturb more than ion concentration: pollutants, pollen, and small particles (called particulates) may be brought down to ground level, and maybe some people are sensitive to these.

3

WEATHER AND BEHAVIOUR

THERE'S A RIOT GOING ON

In the 1989 Spike Lee film *Do the Right Thing* tempers fray as the temperature climbs. The movie depicts one day in a heatwave in Brooklyn as hotheads become hotter, the heat of the day culminating in a riot provoked by seemingly not much at all other than the weather.

Several studies have found a relationship between high temperature and increased aggressive behaviour. In the United States, crime of all sorts increases on hot days, particularly violent crime (murder, assault, robbery, and rape). In agreement with this finding, violent crime is more common in the warmer southern states – in contrast, non-violent crime is less common further south. A similar pattern has been found in France, Spain, and Italy, countries with large north to south variations. The frequency of civil conflicts in the period 1950–2004 in tropical regions is related to the El Niño and La Niña phenomena, with conflicts being twice as likely in El Niño years. The El Niño is the warm phase of the ENSO, the El Niño Southern Oscillation, when a large area of warm water develops in the eastern equatorial Pacific coast off South America, leading to increasing temperatures in the region, as well as drought in some areas. These events happen every three to seven years, and last around a year or longer.

The corresponding cold phase is called the La Niña, and civil conflicts in the region are less common during these events.

As you might guess by now, it isn't clear what the real reason for this relationship is. There are probably several. When it's cold people are less likely to go out and engage in social interactions in the streets; in *Do the Right Thing* trouble got going when the crowd congregated. People start drinking more alcohol on hot summer nights, and we know excessive alcohol can fuel violence. Unpleasant conditions increase discomfort and irritability. Heat makes us more aroused and more likely to act.

However, the relationship between temperature and tendency to violence isn't a simple straight line but is instead what we call curvi-linear, broadly in the shape of an inverted U. A study of the number of aggravated assaults in Dallas, a southern city with plenty of hot days to provide data, showed that the number of assaults rises as the temperature rises to approximately 30°C, but as it goes above that, the amount of violence goes down again. It's as though above a certain temperature it's just too darned hot to do anything. We also observe different patterns in the night and day: the number of violent inci-dents is related to the temperature by a simple straight line in the somewhat cooler hours of night. How can we explain these patterns? The best-known account is Baron and Bell's *negative affect escape* (NAE) model, which states that the discomfort caused by moderately high and low temperatures facilitates aggression, but extreme temperatures arouse competing motives, such as a desire to escape, which conflict with and thereby reduce aggression.

We don't observe an increase just in violent crime; the incidence of less drastic aggression, such as road rage, increases too. In one study carried out in Phoenix, Arizona, a researcher sat at a road junction every Saturday from April to August, during which period the tem-perature ranged from 29°C to 42°C (and yes, 29° was the cool end of the study). The researcher sat in her car at the same junction, a single lane controlled by traffic lights, and when the lights turned green she very socially just sat there. The researchers measured the frequency and duration of honks from the cars behind her, and honks became more frequent and lasted longer the hotter the weather. The relationship was linear – the graph of honk number versus temperature forms a straight line. The researchers also noted that the drivers of cars with their windows down honked the most – because, they argued, those cars didn't have air conditioning. Even supposedly friendly games are affected: sportspeople are more cantankerous as the mercury rises, too. Baseball pitchers (throwers) retaliate more when it's hot. A *revenge pitch* is when a pitcher perceives a teammate to have been deliberately hurt by a pitch, and seeks revenge with his or her own throw. The number of revenge pitches increases on hot days. It isn't down to a factor such as hot weather making pitches less accurate because throws are just accurate on hot days as cold days, so on hot days it's cold-blooded revenge. Pitchers retaliated 22% of the time on days that peaked at 13°C, whereas their rate of retaliation rose to 27% when the temperature reached 35°C. The authors of the baseball study suggest two things are going on in hot weather: inhibitions against retaliating are lower, and pitchers are more likely to consider the actions of others as being hostile in intent.

There is mixed news about less pleasant weather: crime goes down when it's raining, but the incidence of domestic violence goes up.

WEATHER AND COGNITION

I find it difficult to concentrate on warm, sunny days; I just want to be outside, enjoying the sunshine. On the other hand I find it difficult to focus when it's snowing because snow is relatively rare and very beautiful. Rainy days have a fascination of their own too, and I am frequently distracted by checking the rainfall total for the day, or at least the hourly rainfall rate. But I am unusually obsessed by the weather and therefore probably not typical. Are there effects of the weather on cognition in the general population?

In general gloomy weather lowers our mood, which helps us focus more and think more deeply. Some studies have found that memory is better on cloudy, rainy days than sunny days. One typical study tested the ability of Australian shoppers to recall the identity and location of several small items (e.g., model cars, a piggy bank) placed at random places in a small shop; the design was an "ambush" study, where randomly selected participants were stopped on leaving the store, across different times and with therefore different weather conditions. The researchers found that shoppers could recall on average three times as many items on cloudy days than sunny days. The proposed mechanism is that mood might be better on sunny days. There are then several reasons why good mood might lead to worse memory: people might be less motivated to remember, either preferring simply to hurry up and get on with enjoying themselves or worrying that putting a lot of effort into remembering something will spoil their good mood. Different moods might lead us to engage in different types of cognitive processing, with one prominent proposal being that negative mood makes us focus on bottom-up processing, while positive mood encourages us to focus on top-down processing. Emphasis on bottom-up processing might be more advantageous in simple memory tasks. It's all a bit speculative.

In general the effects are complex and several things are most likely going on. The meteorological variables that have the greatest effect on mood and memory are hours of sunshine, temperature, and humidity. High levels of humidity lowered scores on concentration tasks and increased reports of sleepiness. Rising temperatures lowered anxiety. The number of hours of sunshine predicts how optimistic we are. Pleasant weather, with higher temperature and higher barometric pressure, results in better mood, better memory, and "broadened" cognitive style, leading to people being more open and creative. However, these effects are found only during the spring and depend on the amount of time spent outside – as you might expect, the more time you spend outside, the greater the effect of these meteorological variables on how you think. Perhaps in line with the research on seasonal affective disorder, we might observe these effects only in spring because people have been deprived of pleasant weather in the winter, and it's the contrast that's important.

In summer cloudy days help us think more clearly in a focused way, perhaps because our mood is slightly lower, while sunny weather improves creativity and receptivity to new ideas. The lack of sunlight associated with rainy days also causes serotonin levels to dip, and as serotonin levels decrease, carbohydrate cravings increase, so we become hungrier for starchy foods on cloudy days. Excessive carbohydrate consumption promotes production of the amino acid tryptophan, which increases tiredness, thereby lowering concentration. So your concentration might benefit from your slightly lower mood on cloudy days, but that benefit will be lost if you try to compensate by eating carbs.

The weather also affects what we value. The researcher Uri Simonsohn has studied how weather affects college admissions. One study looked at 682 university applicants and how the weather affected the way interviewers perceived them: on cloudy days the interviewers had a preference for applicants with strong academic profiles, while on sunny days non-academic attributes, such as being an athlete or taking part in extra-curricular activities, were taken much more into account. As Simonsohn says, clouds make nerds look good. It works both ways: on cloudy days applicants are more likely to prefer institutions with strong academic records at the cost of non-academic strengths. Simonsohn examined the behaviour of 1,284 prospective students at a college known for its "academic strengths and recreational weaknesses", which is a nice and kind way of putting it. Cloud cover increased the probability of enrolment, by quite a margin: an increase in cloudiness on a particular day by one standard deviation led to almost a 10% increase in the number of applications. Of course the students didn't consciously reason "It's cloudy – I like this place"; the mechanism of action is presumably through non-conscious priming of academic activities – sunshine makes you think of the advantages of being outside, while dull days make you think about being indoors studying. Which university you go to has massive effects on your subsequent life, and I find it rather frightening that our lives might be determined by how cloudy it is on a particular day.

Given these findings, it is not surprising that the weather should have effects on schooling. Although I know of no data on the subject, it is probably the case that children find it easier to concentrate and remember things slightly better on cloudy days. There is some evidence that falling barometric pressure increases misbehaviour, and we get rapidly falling pressure when it is going to rain, is raining, and if the depression is still approaching, when it's very windy. There is an old lay belief that falling pressure affects the blood flow to the brain, but this belief isn't supported by any evidence. As boys are generally more likely to misbehave (or at least be caught), anything influencing naughtiness might be more apparent with boys.

THE WEATHER AND CREATIVITY

Nobel laureates are not randomly distributed across the globe. The Dutch psychologist Evert Van de Vliert has observed that there are disproportionately more of them towards the poles and around the equator. Countries such as the US, Britain, Scandinavia (particularly Sweden), Russia, Western European countries, Australia, and New Zealand do very well. Britain, for example, with a population of around 60 million, had 120 laureates by 2013.

You might think that such inequality is not surprising, and simply reflects income and poverty, but it is possible to use statistical techniques to remove the effect of these variables. The inequality in distribution remains, and yes, it is due to climate and the weather.

Van de Vliert has been interested in what underlies creativity in general, and has used several indicators, including the number of patents generated by a country, as well as the number of Nobel Prize laureates per capita. He has speculated that extremes are important: cold stress and heat stress promote creativity, *as long as the society has the resources to promote research*. Cold and heat promote creativity in wealthier populations, but hinder it in poorer populations, controlling as much as possible for several other variables, including intellectualisation (those IQ differences between counties), industrialisation, and urbanisation. As we have observed, climate also affects the spread of human-to-human parasites, which are much more common in hotter climates, and which have an effect on creativity. As might be expected, differences in creativity across the wold are moderated by thermal climate, wealth resources, and parasite load. The amount of precipitation (whether it's a dry or wet climate) doesn't seem to matter.

The data suggest that sunshine is associated with creativity. We find that in the US, studies have shown that the value of patents correlates with the annual sunshine average of the region. These are rather coarse measures of both creativity and weather, but they are suggestive. Furthermore creatively successful people tend to move to sunnier climates, which is perhaps far from surprising, but those who do then experience an increase in their creativity. In contrast, those who relocate to less sunny places experience a decrease in output. As a specific example (and we should be wary in general of specific examples) we might note the outpouring of creativity of the French post-impressionist artist Paul Gauguin, who moved to French Polynesia for much of the last ten years of his life.

Not everyone agrees that sunshine is good for creativity. We have noted that sunshine is bad for focused cognition, and some researchers are adamant that sunshine is just as bad for creativity. The economic anthropologist Adam Alter argues that sunshine makes us less reflective, less likely to take risks, and less creative. Sunshine turns us – or at least many of us – into sun-seeking zombies. As Alter points out, when the warm sunshine comes out, we don't think about buckling down to the hard work that's the basis of creativity, but of heading to the beach or lying on the grass. Hard work and creativity make us feel good in the way that sunshine does, and is a substitute for sunshine, not a result of it.

These contradictory findings can be explained because they are *generalisations* – we all have different cognitive styles and, as we saw in our examination of how weather influences mood, different preferences. A sun-lover is likely to be affected very differently by a heatwave from someone who detests hot, sunny weather; the first sort of people might give up work and head for the beach, while the latter might shut themselves in a cool dark room and compose a great symphony. I know a famous researcher who spent a sabbatical in southern California, and hated it. He did some of the best work of his life in air-conditioned gloom while there. On the other hand

I spent some time in San Diego and got much, much less done than I had anticipated. Goethe complained that "excellent personalities", modestly including his own, "suffer most from the adverse effects of the atmosphere". Handel and Mahler were also affected by the seasons, producing many of their great works in autumn and spring.

The seasons and climate can affect the content of creative work. It is difficult to imagine Gauguin's pictures of Polynesia carrying the same power if he had not actually been there. Similarly Cézanne's landscapes scream intense, bleaching French sunshine. Van Gogh's artworks were swayed by the seasons, being dominated by ominous clouds and darkness in the winter months, and showing more optimistic sunshine, light, and the stars during the summer months. Some argue that his bold, aggressive brushstrokes laden with paint were more frenzied in the winter months, while his summer pictures were less intense.

WORKING, STOCK MARKETS, AND SHOPPING

Given these differences, it is perhaps not surprising that workers are more productive when the weather is bad. One impressive study examined employee productivity in a bank in Japan, an online workforce in the US, and performance in a laboratory experiment. All showed that people work more and better when the weather isn't so good compared with a nice, sunny, warm day. The researchers argued that there are more distractions in good weather; workers spend time and effort wishing they were enjoying the sun rather than the task that should have been at hand. This idea that for many people cognitive distractibility increases on nice days is a recurrent one with strong explanatory powers. The authors of this study suggest that not all is hopeless; they argue that where possible managers should assign work that requires more sustained attention on wet days, and work that allows more flexibility on sunny days. Most people and most jobs, however, don't give you any choice.

It's also been observed that even when you control for possible confounds, stock market returns are slightly higher in warm, sunny weather. It's thought that people are more willing to take risks, and consequently benefit from higher returns. A 2003 study by Hishleifer and Shumway found that sunshine (and only sunshine) was strongly correlated with stock market returns taken from 26 stock markets over 15 years. Note that this behaviour is irrational: sunshine might have a minor effect on some agricultural industries and ice cream production, but the size of the effect seems too big in western industrial societies. It appears that sunshine raises mood a little, and people misattribute this elevation of mood to being optimistic about life in general because the conditions in the world are good. And if the world is in a good place, it makes sense to invest. After you control for sunshine, other weather variables have no effect on stock market returns. This sort of research emphasises first how irrational we are when making complex decisions, and second how we don't think we're irrational, but attribute our beliefs to something more plausible.

The good news for employers is that few weather variables appear to affect how hard their employees try to work. One study showed that the only variable that affected the performance of data input clerks (it was the late 1970s) was a "discomfort index" combining temperature and humidity – people quickly feel uncomfortable in hot, humid conditions. The experiment was carried out in Birmingham, Alabama, and it isn't clear whether the office was air-conditioned. In fact many things aren't clear about this self-admittedly pilot study, so the results should be treated with caution. It is possible that a larger study would show that other factors do have an effect – we know for example that industrial accidents are more likely before a thunderstorm, which would presumably have a dramatic effect on productivity. The range of accidents that can happen to clerks is rather limited. In general it seems that warm, sunny weather decreases what is called our natural risk aversiveness, most people's general reluctance to take risks. While some people take risks and end up in a fight, others take risks on the market. Some have argued that there's some evolutionary benefit to risk taking in good weather, although what that might be isn't clear; perhaps the consequences of making a mistake were less bad for our ancestors. Perhaps. We also need to explain why speculation on the stock market in fine weather tends to pay off – obviously not all risks are good. Clearly something else is going on here; maybe people are more creative in their investments. We don't know.

It's not surprising that the weather can influence our shopping behaviour; of course what we buy is going to be influenced by the climate and weather. There isn't a big demand for raincoats in the Sahara, and few people rush to buy ice cream when it's snowing. Rain increases the sale of umbrellas (I only ever buy them when it's raining, and lose them as soon as the rain stops), and in a heatwave as the temperature soars so does the sale of salad and barbecue food. The weather, though, influences our general shopping behaviour. It seems that sunshine makes us feel more positive and spend more: when the sun is out, people want to shop. One study analysed sales figures from a tea and coffee shop and compared them with the weather over the same period: sales were clearly related to sunshine. Another study exposed some participants to artificial sunlight, and found that these participants said that they were more willing than a control group to buy things from a rather strange list, including green tea, gym membership, newspaper subscriptions, and plane tickets.

This was the finding of a three-part study. In the first study, the investigators analysed sales figures from a retail store that sold tea and tea-related products. They had data across six years of daily sales and daily weather conditions. In the second study, the researchers had participants complete a daily survey, which assessed their mood, how much tea and coffee they bought and consumed, and their total expenses for the day. Participants recorded this information for 20 days in March. The third study manipulated participants' exposure to artificial sunlight, assessed their mood, and questioned their willingness to pay for five products: green tea, juice, a gym membership, an airline ticket, and a newspaper subscription. The researchers concluded that sunshine makes us feel more positive and, in turn, shop more.

Personally I find these results surprising: I can think of few things I'd rather do on a sunny day than go into a sunless store and spend money. On the other hand, looking around the mall near my local gym, it's clear that heavy rain can put people off from going out at all. And that's another likely factor in why people shop more when the weather's fine: people are just more likely to go out.

The nature of shopping is changing, first with a shift to out-of-town shopping and then from physical to online shopping. There is less research on the weather and online shopping, but the data suggests that the reverse happens with online shopping: when the weather's nice, online sales go down. The explanation is probably partly the same, in that when it's nice, people go outdoors, away from their computers. Conversely when it rains, people spend more online, but the extent to which they do so depends on the location. You find more online spending in Marseilles on a wet day than on Paris, probably because people are more used to inclement weather in Paris, and therefore less put off going outside.

DAYLIGHT SAVINGS

In spring many regions of the world, particularly in the north, put their clocks one hour forward early in spring, and then put them back one hour in mid-autumn. This shift is called daylight savings time (DST) in the US and other areas, and British summer time in the UK. The rationale is that we shift an hour of daylight from the beginning of the day, where we don't need it (few are up and about and gardening at 5 a.m.), to the evening, where we can enjoy a glass of wine outside in the setting sun after a hard day's work. It is a change easily remembered by "spring forward, fall back". There is also the rationale that summer time saves resources; few need electric lights and heating early in the morning, but a bit of light later in the evening saves energy. It is no coincidence that daylight savings was first widely adopted in Europe in the Great War. Germany, Austria-Hungary, and the UK all started a form of daylight savings in 1916, the belief being that summer time conserved resources.

There have been occasional deviations from normal daylight savings. During the Second World War, from 1941 to 1945, Britain was on *double summer time*, with the winter on summer time and the summer on double summer time, two hours ahead of GMT, again supposedly to spare resources and give more light at the end of the day. I grew up in a period when the UK experimented with British standard time, when the UK stayed on permanent summer time from 1968 to 1971. My memory of that period is that it was perpetually dark. Unfortunately permanent summer time did not mean permanent summer, and the House of Commons on a free vote in December 1970 decided to end the experiment by a large majority.

The British standard time experiment did allow for an analysis of the effects. As you might expect, dark mornings mean more traffic accidents, and this pattern was indeed what was found. On the other hand, substantially fewer accidents and fatalities occurred in the evenings. Overall it was estimated that about 1,000 lives were saved each year in road traffic accidents. However, the UK implemented much more stringent drink-driving laws and checks at the same time, and because people are more likely to consume alcohol in the evening than morning, some or even all of the savings might have been due to this change.

The British Royal Society for the Prevention of Accidents currently campaigns for a return to the wartime summer time and double summer time system, on the grounds that the lighter evenings would result in more saved lives. The proposal is opposed by people who work outside, and people who live further north. We in Scotland are firmly against the idea: it is bad enough when sunrise is around 9 a.m., but 10 a.m. is an unimaginably grim prospect. And that's sunrise, not when the sun actually manages to peek over the hills.

In any case it is not obvious that permanent summer time would save lives. As we have seen, the 1968–1971 savings might have been due to something else entirely. It is also not the case that daylight savings saves as many resources as believed. Adam Alter has observed that much research has shown that daylight savings has ways of increasing consumption rather than reducing it – for example, by increasing the use of air conditioning, which is a voracious consumer of energy.

But most importantly fiddling with time and our body clocks is not good for us. When the clocks change our body clocks have to change too, and that has significant costs, particularly when we lose an hour of sleep in the spring. The effect is the same as giving a nation jet lag, and we all know how bad and unhealthy jet lag is. Adam Alter reports that the road accident rate increases by 7% the day after the change. The US stock market usually fares relatively badly the first business day after the change for no other apparent reason. It takes most people a day or two to adjust, so the increase in accident rates almost certainly lingers.

There might be less obvious but longer-lasting and even more disruptive effects. It has been claimed that daylight savings affects education by putting children and students out of phase with their natural biorhythms for several months of the year. After all, non-daylight savings time is more related to the natural time, so daylight savings is like putting children on permanent jet lag. This claim might sound far-fetched, but there is strong evidence for it. The state of Indiana in the US provides a very neat way of testing these sorts of ideas because some counties in the state observe daylight savings, but not all, which must be very confusing for the local inhabitants, particularly those living near county borders. But given that the only thing that differs between these counties is whether they observe daylight savings (it's a relatively small geographical area without any other substantial differences between counties, such as income, and some of the schools compared are just a few miles apart), Indiana provides a nice test of the effects of daylight savings. Research shows that students in areas that observe daylight savings score 16 points lower on the SAT (originally standing for "Scholastic Aptitude Test") than fellow students nearby in areas that observe standard time all year. Sixteen points is a huge difference; vast sums of money are spent trying to eliminate much smaller regional differences. The researchers Gaski and Gagarin dramatically concluded in 2011 that "DST appears to cause brain damage".

So the psychological evidence suggests that we should indeed abolish daylight savings and British summer time, but instead of introducing BST all year round, we should stick with natural time, and have GMT all year round. The price of more barbies finishing in the evening gloaming in the south would be a small one to pay.

WEATHER AND VOTING

In many countries where voting is not compulsory the turnout at elections can be surprisingly, some say disappointingly, small. In the UK the turnout among eligible voters has gradually declined from a turnout of 83.9% of those eligible to vote in 1950 to 68.7% in 2017; in the US the distribution of turnout over time is more complex, falling to 61.4% in 2016, the lowest since 1996, but the Obama years were marked by high turnouts.

Studies in the US, Spain, and the Netherlands found that wet weather systematically reduces voter turnout, with an estimate that for every 25 mm (about an inch) of rain that falls, turnout is reduced by 1 percentage point. A 2004 study suggested that the value was somewhat larger, with 5% of the turnout being affected by the weather: a reasonable but hardly large amount. A Dutch study found that very sunny weather pushed up turnout by 1%. The effect might be volatile: a subsequent study in Sweden failed to replicate these findings, and the British election expert Professor John Curtice has examined the relationship between voting patterns and weather in all the UK general elections between 1922 and 2010 and found no relationship. February 1974 was the coldest election day recorded (and very wet too), yet voter turnout went up to a very respectable 78.8%.

There is a widespread belief in the UK that rain slightly favours the Conservative Party while warm, sunny weather slightly favours the Labour Party, but there is little evidence to support this belief. There is a similar belief in the same direction in the US, that rain favours the right, but again little evidence to support it, although some have claimed that weather affected the results of the 1960 and 2000 presidential elections; election day in 1960 was very dry across the US, and election day in 2000 was wet in Florida. There is some evidence that the weather has differentially affected turnout in Spain, with high turnout hurting the more right-wing parties more; however, in Spain the beneficiaries of the higher turnout were not the more left-wing parties but miscellaneous smaller parties. The supposed mechanism behind these findings is that voters of higher socioeconomic status are more likely to vote for right-of-centre parties, and they are less dependent on public transport and less likely to be deterred by poor weather. You can imagine if support for one party is more wavering than for the other, bad weather might push some people over the edge and, if they're not that bothered, stop them turning out. However, as the population has generally become wealthier, and most people have cars, it's possible that there was an effect decades ago which is no longer observed.

Of course exceptionally severe weather might interfere with the turnout, but British elections tend to be in late spring or early summer, or occasionally autumn, and American elections in November, when the weather is usually not too extreme. But again some caution is necessary in guessing what people might do: Hurricane Sandy caused great disruption around New York just before the 2012 presidential election, but there was no effect on voting. One possibility here is that disadvantaged groups saw the election as particularly important, and were therefore exceptionally resilient in their behaviour. The weather interacts with our intentions and behaviour in complex ways.

SPRING FLINGS

When Christmas passes and the winter comes to an end, the daffodils come out, the lambs gambol, and a young man's fancy turns to fancying. It's a cliché, but is there any support for the notion, and is it just the fancy of young men that's affected? Apparently not: one study in France found that women were more likely to say yes to an offer of a date from an "attractive" stranger on sunny days compared to cloudy days, with the figures being 22% and 14% (acceptance rates which seem high to me whatever the weather). The researchers argued that sunny weather led to better mood, leading to people being more generous in their opinions.

On the whole, though, most of the research has rather surprisingly concluded that it's cold weather that makes the sap rise. In 2004 and 2005 two Polish researchers approached 100 heterosexual men and asked them about their views on female attractiveness by rating pictures of silhouetted women in swimsuits and female breasts of various sizes. Exactly the same images were rated higher in winter than summer. The best explanation is that testosterone levels peak in winter. A study of 1,548 men living in Tromsø, in north Norway, found that testosterone levels were lowest when the temperature was highest and the length of daylight longest; there were two peaks of testosterone, both in fall and winter months, one in February, and the largest peak in October and November. The differences were large, with levels varying by over 30%. These seasonal variations are very sensitive to geography, with the same researchers finding no seasonal variation among 915 men living in San Diego, which has much less pronounced temperature and daylight variations.

We do not yet know why testosterone levels vary seasonally in regions with wide seasonal variations in temperature and length of daylight, but we do know that high levels of testosterone lead to more sexual activity, so unsurprisingly there is a peak in the number of births nine months after the peak in testosterone levels. Given the testosterone peak is in fall, this means the birth peak occurs in summer. One evolutionary possibility is that this mechanism ensures that babies are born at a time of plenty, while in southern latitudes the year-round abundance means that regulation of time of birth is less important. In fact conceptions go down during heatwaves – perhaps sex is less appealing when it's too darned hot. Some recent studies suggest that the length of day is more important in influencing conception in the north, and temperature in the south.

Although this explanation sounds plausible, there are contradictory findings that show that the picture is much more complicated. Other studies have shown that seasonal variations in births are stronger in hotter climates. Another study did find a pronounced seasonal variation in birth rates, in that in warmer southern US states, such as Louisiana and Georgia, birth rates were much lower in April and May, and much higher in August, September, and October. In Louisiana, for example, birth rates were 45% higher in the summer months, which is a dramatic difference. These results are consistent with the idea that conception rates are higher in winter, but inconsistent with the idea that seasonal variations in testosterone are the only thing going on. Several other possibilities come to mind, such as people spending more time indoors or spending more time together, or perhaps sex is just something to do when the weather isn't so great outside. These seasonal variations, though, are declining in strength over time in hot areas, presumably because people are on average spending less time outside, and air conditioning reduces the effect of outside heat and humidity. There is some evidence, though, that seasonal variations in conception are increasing in more northerly, colder regions, for reasons that aren't at all well understood.

It isn't just sex and conception that are affected by the weather and climate. One general finding of psychology that has been particularly demonstrated within social psychology in recent years is how sensitive we are to many influences, many of them outside our awareness. These effects go under the general name of *social priming*. The classic finding is that thinking about being old makes healthy young students walk more slowly, although this finding has been disputed, with social priming results at the centre of the supposed current *replicability crisis* in psychology. With such sensitivity to the outside world, it is hardly surprising that our love life is affected by the weather. Another important development is called *embodied cognition*, an approach that emphasises the way in which the mind is grounded in the body, and in turn the world. So when we think about using a tool, such as a hammer, brain imaging shows that the parts of the brain that would light up if we actually used the hammer become active just by thinking about doing so. Meteorological variables act upon us in just the same way.

In one experiment, student participants met an experimenter in the lobby and travelled up in the lift together to the main psychology rooms. As they did so the experimenter asked the student to hold the experimenter's cup for him or her while he or she jotted down the student's details. The cup contained either hot or iced coffee. As you might guess from the discussion of social priming and embodied cognition, students who held the hot cup later rated the experimenter as more friendly – "warmer" – than those who held the cold cup.

Being warm appears to make us think more warmly of people and the world. Similar experiments have shown that just holding something cold can make you feel lonelier, and people who feel socially excluded crave warm drinks and food. So extending these results, being warm will make people feel socially warmer and friendlier, and more likely to interact with other. Researchers have concluded that social warmth and physical warmth are to some extent interchangeable, so warm climates might lead to more warm personalities, more warm interaction, and more romance. It's therefore no surprise that romantic films are more popular when it's warm (and in contrast comedy films are more popular when it's cold, as people want to be cheered – warmed – up).

It isn't just love that is affected by the weather; it also influences how nice we are. As we might expect from the embodied cognition results, people are more helpful when the weather is nice; psychologists say that they're more *prosocial*. One study showed that drivers in France are more likely to pick up hitchhikers when it's sunny than when it's cloudy. Some studies have found that tipping goes up when it's sunny, although other studies have found no effect. Even participants in experiments and interviews are more helpful when the weather is better. These studies show that it's fine weather in general, not just sunshine, that's important in acting prosocially, and the effects of heat can be offset by high humidity.

4

WEATHER AND BELIEF

WEATHER AND THE DIVINE

Our understanding of the weather and climate is now extraordinarily sophisticated, and we understand the chain of physical mechanisms involved between fluctuations in the jet stream over North America a few days ago and the downpour over your head today. In the past things were of course different, but even today we talk about freak weather events as being included among "acts of God", a clause which may be used to exclude those events from payouts by insurers. In 1969 Betty Penrose of Arizona sued God for $100,000 damages after He allowed lightning to strike and damage her house; she won the case by default as God didn't turn up to the court, but it wasn't much help because He continued to ignore the case and didn't pay up.

Without scientific models the weather is terrifying, so it is not surprising that pre-scientific peoples sought to understand and control the weather. The ancient Greeks and Romans of course tried to understand aspects of the weather by turning them into deities: Anemoi, the winds; Eos, dawn; Horae, seasons; Iris, rainbows; and Zephyris, the West Wind, to name but a few, under the control of Zeus and Hera. Zeus of course would hurl thunderbolts, an infinite number made by the Cyclops and stored in a bucket, and so powerful that they could even be thrown at other gods to put them in their place. Myths surrounding the weather show how humans struggle to make sense of and control the environment in a pre-scientific mode of thought.

Children also think pre-scientifically. I was terrified of thunder and lightning as a child, partly because of the explanations I was given of their occurrence. I am sure my parents and grandparents were trying to be helpful in telling me that thunder was the sound of angry angels stamping their feet on clouds, or God being upset with my bad behaviour, but Mum, it really didn't help. Such arguments were convincing to the young me, but now we view them as examples of *magical thinking*, where people give elaborate explanations linking two phenomena that just appear to be related (my being naughty followed by a thunderstorm). At least my father's explanation of thunder being the sound of clouds rubbing together was less personal and in fact nearer to the truth.

FEAR OF THE WEATHER

Given this background, it's not surprising that when I was a child, as soon as the lightning flashed and the thunder rolled, I would run home at once. Fortunately I grew out of this fear and went to the other extreme, becoming fascinated by thunderstorms and seeking them out, but some people never lose this fear; they suffer from *astraphobia* (fear of thunder and lightning) or perhaps just *brontophobia* (fear of thunder). Astraphobia is one of the most common *phobias*, or fear of specific things. It's no joke: phobias can be very debilitating, interfering with ordinary life, and in the case of a fear of natural events the phobia can become generalised to *agoraphobia*, a general fear of open spaces and being outside – after all, in some places you can never be quite certain when a thunderstorm might happen. Phobias produce symptoms of anxiety, with elevated heart rate, sweating, inability to think clearly, nausea, crying, shaking, and the feelings of panic and dread. Fortunately phobias are one of the more straightforward psychological disorders to treat, usually responding well to cognitive behavioural treatments, such as desensitisation (exposing the person to a some very short, gentle thunderclaps to show nothing bad happens, and gradually turning up the volume and duration).

I may no longer suffer from astraphobia, but I do suffer from mild *ancraophobia* (fear of the wind). Wind can be a power destructive force, but can also be mildly disruptive: if you live in the country in particular you may worry about telephone and electricity lines coming down. Although I don't like strong winds, the fear doesn't interfere with my life (much), and therefore doesn't require treatment. People with *chionophobia* have an irrational fear of snow; I love snow, as do many, particularly around Christmas, but I do have a somewhat irrational and overstated fear of being prevented from getting home because of the snow.

It should be pointed out that if you surf the Web for lists of bizarre phobias, you will find plenty, and plenty of weather ones. Many of them are made up, however; they are hypothetical names, constructed from pseudo-Greek to answer such important questions as what would an irrational fear of rainbows be called (*iridophobia* it turns out). I made fear of rainbows up, feeling safe that no one has claimed to have suffered from it, but on checking, how wrong I was. Of course you don't know whether people are making it up, but one plausible-sounding account said that she was afraid of them because rainbows are "mysterious and weird . . . the way they evaporate . . . they're huge, they look like they are watching you". Such accounts, though, are anecdotal, and I have been unable to find any clinical case studies of iridophobia.

Phobias are a kind of anxiety disorder, and are very common: it is estimated that between 1 in 20 and 1 in 10 people suffer from one or more. They arise when we become conditioned to respond with fear and aversion to some stimulus, such as a snake, wasp, or spider (or a rainbow). In what is called *classical conditioning* an aversive *unconditioned stimulus*, such as a wasp sting, is paired with the sight and sound of a wasp (the *conditioned stimulus*), leading to a *conditioned response* (fear of the sound of a wasp). We can acquire fear vicariously: if a young child sees her mother exhibiting extreme fear of a spider the child might develop the same phobia. We have to explain why some people are susceptible to developing phobias and others aren't; the answer lies in slight abnormalities of the brain, particularly an area of the brain known as the *limbic system*, which plays an important role in emotional processing.

Some phobias are more common than others, and these tend to be ones for which it makes some sense to be afraid of the thing or idea: snakes, heights, spiders, blood, and strangers being common examples. Research shows that primates learn to be afraid of snakes much more easily than of other things. It seems that we have a tendency to be afraid of certain potentially dangerous stimuli, but in phobias that fear is taken too far.

Some weather events are candidates for things of which it is logical to be a bit afraid, and therefore we should perhaps not be surprised that astraphobia and brontophobia occur.

WEATHER AND FOLK SAYINGS

Knowledge about the weather gets distilled into folk sayings, or proverbs. "Red sky at night, shepherd's delight; red sky in the morning, shepherd's warning". These sayings are *heuristics* – they give us fast and easy access to knowledge about the weather without having to run a massive computer simulation every time we see a beautiful red sunset. The cost of using heuristics is that they are not always right; I remember plenty of red sunsets that have been followed by miserable days. The use of weather sayings exemplifies how we use statistical or *distributional information*: we are exposed to many examples, and from them abstract a central underlying tendency. This process reduces the memory load and enables us to predict the future. What's more, with folk sayings we can distil our cultural experience, in that we might not have observed many red skies at night, but the population across history has. Weather proverbs are very popular, with recent research by the UK Met Office finding that nearly three quarters of the sample surveyed used these sayings.

Most weather folk sayings have at least an element of truth in them – no doubt a manifestation of the selection of the fittest in folk memory for proverbs, in that if they weren't useful, no one would remember them. Here are a few.

"Dew is on the grass, rain will never come to pass". Dew forms in still nights under clear skies, which we get with high pressure, when fronts are kept at bay and rain is unlikely. However, "never" is a bad word to use when talking about the weather.

"Mackerel skies and mares' tails make tall ships carry low sails". Mares' tails are high cirrus clouds, and a mackerel sky is formed from altocumulus or cirrocumulus clouds. Both are associated with the approach of a warm front, which most likely will bring rain within 12 hours.

"It's too cold for snow" might be true in very cold climates, but generally is not true in the UK. However, it is the case that the lowest temperature records in the UK, such as the −27.2°C recorded at Altnaharra in northern Scotland on the morning of 30 December 1995, occur on clear, windless nights over fresh snow, after the snow has passed.

"Rain before seven, fine before eleven" is widely used, and is supported by the evidence because on many occasions four hours is long enough for a weather front to pass. Like all of these sayings there are exceptions, for some fronts can linger considerably longer: anyone applying the saying in London on the morning of 14 June 1903 would have been in for an unpleasant shock: it rained continuously from late morning on the 13th to late evening on the 15th, a total of 54 hours being recorded at Camden Square, which is the longest period of continuous rainfall in a populated region of the UK in recent times. (Parts of the Northwest Highlands of Scotland have probably seen longer; it rained for 72 hours at Loch Sloy in December 1994.) A total of 183 mm of rain fell at Kew in the middle fortnight of June. It was also very cold, with a maximum of just 10°C on the 19th, which is exceptional for London for June. Anyone applying this saw would have been very disappointed.

"Cows lie down when it's about to rain" is one of the most popular sayings in the UK, but in this case there is no supporting evidence for it. Some beliefs that have no basis in fact just take on a life of their own and persist, perhaps because not enough people take note of the many occasions when cows stand up and it rains, or lie down when it doesn't rain. Humans are not very good at making use of negative evidence.

WHY ARE WE SO INTERESTED IN THE WEATHER?

Oscar Wilde didn't like talking about the weather very much: he made several comments about the conversational failings of those who mention it, the most famous of which was "conversation about the weather is the last refuge of the unimaginative". Yet the stereotype of the British means that when strangers meet the first thing they do is to strike up a conversation – "lovely weather for the time of year, isn't it?"

There is certainly plenty of anecdotal evidence in books and on the Web that people find talking about the weather is an easy social gambit and provides instant empathy with the listeners. I will say to any relative stranger one from my repertoire of "nice day isn't it", "lovely day today" (better than nice), "not so good today", and "nasty day today" (worse than not so good). A study conducted by Onepoll surveyed 5,000 British adults and found that talking about the weather is the most characteristic trait of the British (with second being sarcasm and third being an ability to queue). And according to the BBC, 94% of British people have mentioned the weather in the last six hours, and 38% have talked about it in the last hour. As social anthropologist Kate Fox observes, these figures suggest that at any moment about a third of the British population is either just about to talk about the weather, currently doing so, or just about to. The British weather is very interesting, as weather goes; our climate is moderated by the Gulf Stream, the jet stream is often over us, and being maritime and at the edge of a continent, it's highly changeable. As I write, the last six weeks have seen a new record low maximum temperature set for Britain and the long-standing April high maximum just failing to be broken. In the last few days we have gone from sun-bathing in the heat to shivering in the rain. There's plenty to talk about. And as Fox says, there is more to words than their content; talking about the weather is a kind of social grooming. Talking about the weather is the modern equivalent of picking nits off your neighbour.

There is a widespread and strongly held belief that the British think and talk about the weather more than other nationalities, but I know of no data to support this assertion. One BBC site claims that people from countries such as Finland talk about the weather less because it is so much less variable; they know it's going to be cold and snowy for five months, so what is there to say? But in my experience people outside Britain do talk about the weather. The US even has a successful television channel devoted to the weather, which Britain does not. Australians use weather as an online search term more than they do sex. It seems that people across the world are obsessed by the weather.

I am often asked why are the British so obsessed with the weather. If you believe what the press says about us, we are a nation obsessed by weather. The press is definitely obsessed, for in the middle of a pretty average winter I open my digital pages of the newspaper to be warned that severe winter weather is heading our way, with some snow (presumably of the wrong sort) and temperatures "as low as −7 C in sheltered parts of rural Scotland". Snow, even in the south of England, is not that rare, and −7 is definitely nippy, but nevertheless unexceptional. Doubtless we will be told that parts of Scotland will be "colder than parts of the former Soviet Union", or some other carefully chosen location, tomorrow.

A much quoted finding is that a 2010 survey for Fox's book *Watching the English* found that 94% of British people (surveyed) had discussed the weather in the last six hours, and 38% in the last 30 minutes. These figures seem large, but without comparison figures we cannot conclude very much. Perhaps the Austrians talk about it even more. Perhaps 97% of people have talked about avocados in the last six hours. Other nations think that Britain is more obsessed with the weather than most: a 2014 survey for British Airways found that "talking about the weather" was one of the attributes most associated with the British. Data, presumably from computers, shows that over half the UK online population visits weather sites every month, with minutes online tripling over the summer. Further survey data shows that perhaps surprisingly the 25–44 age online group is most likely to check the forecast, with women more likely to check than men.

However, comparative data suggests that the American perception may be wrong: more online Americans check their forecast and spend longer doing so than Britons. In this case the stereotype is not immediately supported by the data, although ideally we need information from more countries. My limited experience of travelling the world suggests that people from other countries talk about the weather to the same extent as us: in France and Spain it is always hotter or colder, wetter or drier, cloudier or sunnier than usual (a point to which I will return).

So people talk about the weather across the world because weather satisfies several criteria for being a good thing to chat about wherever you are: it's a good ice breaker; it's uncontroversial; it's impersonal. It's difficult to offend someone when you're just talking about what nice weather it is (or not) for the time of year. And it's easy for the other person to respond without giving offence, and as such, talking about the weather is a form of social grooming. These hunches are supported by surveys: in one survey, 12% of English people commented that keeping the conversation to the weather ensured that conversations stay safe and impersonal. Not always though: in an online survey for Walkers Crisps, a quarter of Britons admitted to becoming defensive if our climate was ridiculed. The British weather might be mediocre, but we're proud of it.

WEATHER OBSERVERS AND STORM CHASERS

There is a difference between talking casually about the weather, being interested in it even, and being obsessed by it, and a lot of people are obsessed by it, me included.

I have been obsessed by the weather since I was 4 and woke up to find the garden covered with thick snow; it was beautiful and amazing. For as long as I can remember I have wanted to record the weather, but it was only when I got a job and settled down in a stable location with a garden that could be an observing station that I really got going. You don't need much to keep fairly decent records: a maximum–minimum thermometer that you can position out of the sun, a rain gauge, and a barometer; this equipment can now be purchased relatively cheaply and easily online or at a garden centre. As with all hobbies you can spend much more time and money, adding humidity metres, anemometers to measure wind speed, sunshine recorders, and complete weather stations that transmit wirelessly to your computer (which is what I now have). Doing it properly is expensive and time-consuming; the British Met Office uses platinum resistance thermometers calibrated every eight years, backed up by liquid-in-glass thermometers to provide a check, with the thermometers positioned 1.25 m above grass housed in a *Stevenson screen*, which prevents sunshine and direct heating of the thermometer, but with slats providing plenty of ventilation, in an open location. A good Stevenson screen will set you back several hundred pounds. As with any obsession, you can spend a lot of money, and a lot of time.

Our understanding of the weather has until very recently depended on a network of observers at land and sea, but now many of these have been replaced by automatic weather stations, which never oversleep, are never ill, and never go on holiday. Before I bought a weather station that stored measurements I was somewhat reluctant to go away to prevent data being lost, and when I had to I would get a reliable friend in to take the 9 a.m. GMT measurements. People still like to take their own records, and still like to share records and talk about the weather. In the UK the Climate Observers Link (COL) and several online newsgroups and weather forums, such as uk.sci.weather, provide plenty of opportunities to do so.

Who are these weather fanatics? A few years ago I carried out a study of the members of online weather discussion groups. A word of warning: as with all of these types of surveys, you are dependent on who replies and who completes the survey, which might not be representative of the weather-obsessive population at large. But I collected over a hundred responses and have no reason to believe the results are skewed in any way.

The most reported reason for being keen on the weather is an obsession and fascination with extremes. Hobbyists like records, particularly local, regional, and national extremes of temperature and rainfall. We like heatwaves and we like snow. We really love snow; there is nothing more likely to generate a spike in traffic in a weather group than the possibility of snow. But extremes of all sorts get us going.

The most obvious result, though, is that the great majority of weather obsessives (and this is not meant to be a derogatory label) are male, over 95% in fact, a finding which will be confirmed if you look at any online weather group. And respondents say they like to keep records, and take pride in keeping accurate records from their station for long periods of time (and the longer the period the more exciting it is to set a new record). This obsession with records and this male bias give some indication of what is going on. The British developmental psychologist Simon Baron-Cohen has written widely about autism and autistic spectrum disorder (including what used to be called Asperger's syndrome). As the spectrum is a continuum, I hope my weather-obsessive friends do not find it insulting to suggest that the typical obsessed weather recorder is a little more along the spectrum than an average member of the population. In support of this claim, some brave volunteers from my sample took a questionnaire developed by Baron-Cohen, and most scored more highly on autistic traits. It is important to note that this finding does not mean that anyone interested in or even obsessed by the weather is autistic or has anything wrong with them at all! It simply means that people obsessed by the weather tend to have certain other personality traits as well. Baron-Cohen theorises that the attention to detail and the search for patterns in many apparently disparate records have evolutionary advantages. He calls it *hyper-systemising*. The possible advantages are shown beautifully by keen weather recorders: weather is a natural phenomenon and the ability of some people to be able to predict it would obviously confer an advantage on that individual and indeed his or her tribe.

But I mostly just observe the weather; I let it come to me. Others are less patient and go to find the weather. The US in particular is famous for storm chasers, who go out looking for extreme thunderstorms and tornadoes in "tornado alley", a region of the central plains of the Midwest, from Texas through Alabama, Oklahoma, and Kansas to Iowa and Nebraska, and to a lesser extent surrounding areas, in tornado season, which is from March to July, particularly in May and June.

These storms are spectacular and beautiful, and images of tornadoes and multiple lightning strikes sell well. But there is another reason why storm chasing is popular, and that's because of the thrills and the danger. The chases releases adrenalin, and a successful chase activates the brain's reward system. It must be a high like any other dangerous sport, or the thrill of the chase, with the bonus of seeing something else few others have seen.

PEOPLE AND CLIMATE CHANGE

The weather affects us, but do we affect the weather? There is considerable evidence that humanity has been gradually changing the climate, particularly since the industrial revolution, and especially during the second half of the twentieth century.

We can distinguish between weather, which are the short-term atmospheric effects producing temporary phenomena, such as warm and cold fronts and cyclones and anticyclones, from climate, which is the underlying long-term pattern of weather conditions prevailing over a long period of time. Meteorologists usually use the Köppen classification system to describe the climate of an area. The British isles and other parts of Northern Europe fall within the broad temperate climate zone, with the more specific classification of temperature as oceanic, without a dry season, and warm but not hot summers. A vast country such as the US straddles several climate zones, from hot desert in the southwest to cold continental in the north. Climate changes over time as a consequence of many factors, not fully understood, but including the position of the continents, and what are called Milankovitch cycles, which depend on the eccentricity of the earth's orbit, oscillations in the tilt of the earth, and precession, which is a very slow wobble of the earth around its axis of rotation. When conditions are favourable (or unfavourable, depending on your point of view), the earth enters a glacial period, or ice age. The most recent ice age, the Pleistocene, began about 2.6 million years ago.

The earth came out of the Pleistocene ice age into the Holocene period 11,700 years ago, an event which enabled the development of agriculture and civilisation. There is still some debate as to whether we have merely entered another interglacial period, or whether the ice age is truly finished, as ice sheets are still extensive over Antarctica, Greenland, and the Arctic. There have been variations in our climate since: Northern Europe enjoyed the Mediaeval Warm Period from about 950 to 1250 CE, and endured (or again enjoyed, if you were a child skating on the Thames) the Little Ice Age from about 1650 to as late as 1850. Since then the earth's climate has been warming, with a particularly notable increase in the latter half of the twentieth century, giving rise to the notorious hockey-stick curve (so called because of the resemblance of the shape of the graph to a hockey stick).

The important point is that the climate has always been changing. The rate of current change appears to be unprecedented, however, and many believe that the current warming is due to human activity, so the phenomenon is called *anthropogenic climate change* (to avoid the adjective "man-made"). I hope I can be allowed the acronym ACC to spare us that mouthful.

Climate change is a controversial topic because of the strength of opinions on both sides. Most people believe that the climate is changing, that humans are responsible for the change, and that something should be done about it. A few people believe that there is no reliable evidence that the climate is changing. Some people accept that the climate is changing but deny that humans are responsible, and therefore there is no need to act. The feeling is so strong that some advocates of acting upon ACC (anthropogenic climate change) call their opponents "deniers", using strong language that makes us think of Holocaust denial. (I've even seen some people called climate deniers instead of climate *change* deniers, which cannot be right – surely no one denies that we have a climate?) The topic is more than controversial; some of the arguments are very emotional.

As in any argument there are several positions that are commonly adopted. There are the undecided, the don't knows, those who are committed for or against, but not that emotional about it, and those committed for or against and highly emotional about it. The extreme arguments are advocated by the latter groups, and I will mostly be focusing on these people. Let's call them advocates and sceptics to avoid using emotive terms such as "denier"; using an emotive name is one sound psychological mechanism for avoiding a proper argument.

This book is primarily about psychology, and I am a psychologist who happens to be an amateur meteorologist. However, I should declare my hand that I think that the evidence that the earth's climate is warming is overwhelming, and in all likelihood mankind's activities are responsible for this warming through such means as fossil fuels producing greenhouse gases, such as CO_2.

The arguments you hear against anthropogenic climate change are varied. They include: the argument mentioned earlier, that climate is always changing naturally; the temperature record is unreliable (it isn't); any warming stopped in 1998 (it didn't); Antarctica is gaining ice (it isn't – it's losing it at an accelerating rate); we're heading back into an ice age, aren't we? (possibly we would in the long term, but catastrophe beckons in the short); we can adapt (change will be too rapid for most animals and plants to adapt); it's the sun (over recent years the sun has shown a cooling trend; glaciers are growing (they're retreating); one extreme weather event doesn't prove there's global warming (true, but the frequency of extreme weather events is accelerating as predicted); and the experts can't agree, so why should we believe them?

In fact consensus among climate researchers is very high: a recent study of studies of studies suggests that about 97% of researchers think that the climate is changing and that humans are responsible. Depending on how you define consensus, it approaches 100%. This level of consensus is very high; in psychology it is not uncommon to find researchers split 50/50 for and against a particular theory. On the other hand it isn't remarkable; 100% of physicists and chemists would stake their lives on the existence of atoms. And it doesn't mean they're right – at the start of the twentieth century a similar proportion of physicist would have told you that they believed in the aether. Nevertheless, many people are surprised that experts agree so much about ACC – they have the impression from the press and talking to others that they're much more split.

While 97% or more of experts believe in ACC, there is much less consensus in the lay population. There have been many surveys over the years about what the "person on the street" thinks, and while as might be expected the detailed numbers are often different, the broad picture is consistent across these studies. The results depend on exactly what is asked and who is asked; results vary depending on where the person is from and factors such as their political convictions.

There are then several types of people defined by their opinions on ACC. I'll give them names which I hope fairly reflect their amount of knowledge (or at least their academic standing) and position.

The expert believer: The 97% of experts (climate scientists) who believe the climate is changing and that humans are responsible. Included in this number are a small number of unpaid experts who have spent a great deal of time investigating the evidence. It is evident to me that there is a lot of data, that it isn't as simple as you might think or be led to believe, and that if you are really going to understand all the arguments, you need to invest a huge amount of time into studying the discussion and evidence.

The non-expert believer: A large group who believes the experts, perhaps including the majority; who can blame them, for life is short, and surely experts can be trusted?

The don't knows: Those who are a little more sceptical than the non-expert believer. They have heard about misgivings and think that the picture is not quite as clear-cut as some academics lead us to believe, but aren't motivated enough to do anything further about it (even finding out more).

The non-expert non-believers: One recent study has shown that 32%, nearly a third, of adult Americans do not think that there is any consensus among scientists. We know they are wrong on this specific point – there is a strong consensus among experts; but of course the experts could all be wrong.

The expert non-believers: The 3% or so who are highly qualified to have an opinion but who argue either that there isn't any global warming or, mostly, that there is global warming but it isn't proven to be due to human activity.

The sceptics: A small group who truly believes the ACC hypothesis but whose public position is that it is unproven or wrong. Needless to say sceptics have strong economic or political reasons motivating their public views. Often these people will masquerade as experts of some sort; occasionally they may be experts. They are likely to have ulterior motives.

I don't think most informed people would find the position of the experts difficult to understand: the experts are driven by the data and the conclusions of climate models based on the data. What is less easy to understand, and therefore the more interesting point, is the position of the "deniers". They are faced with this mass of evidence and an overwhelming scientific consensus. Why then do they persist with their denial?

Psychologists now know a great deal about why people are bad at reasoning and solving logical problems. We are animals built for quick and dirty action on the basis of probabilities: survival is a balance of acting quickly and getting it right. On the whole you are more likely to survive and get your genes into the gene pool if you decide to run away than to sit down and work out if there's something nearby that you could fashion into a weapon. Hence we are swayed by big numbers, we reason using anchors with which we are familiar, we are swayed by evidence for something rather than looking to disprove the hypotheses, we don't believe that events such as dice rolls are independent of each other, we let emotions influence our reasoning – the list is enormous. But this list of fallacies and biases cannot wholly explain why deniers deny.

Some people know the truth but don't want to admit it. If you're making money out of selling and burning fossil fuel then it might not be good for business to say your first priority is to save the planet. A wiser if more selfish strategy is to deny the problem, say the science is bogus – and hell, maybe say there's an ice age coming that we have to worry about. President Trump famously went one further than just saying that he didn't care and that he thought American jobs were more important: he called climate change a Chinese hoax to destroy American industry. His words fall on fertile ground: one study estimated that 32% of Americans, between 2000 and 2010, thought that there was no scientific consensus on climate change. There is a big political divide, with only 15% of conservative Republicans believing that the climate is warming due to human activity, contrasting with 79% of liberal Democrats. Those figures suggest what is going on for most people: they get their news and opinion from the media, and we know that people listen to, watch, and read media that agree with their political views. In Britain liberals and socialists tend to read the *Guardian* rather than the *Daily Mail*. So most of the population are stuck in a self-reinforcing circle of hearing views and news that support and strengthen their opinions: people hear what they want to hear and disregard the rest, as Simon and Garfunkel said; psychologists call the phenomenon *motivated reasoning*. It's an example of what we call *confirmation bias* in action, big time.

But why does this category of people want to hear this account in the first place? There are several psychological and sociological accounts, and they all sound plausible. If you look at the demographics people believe what they have investment in. But there is also a large gender difference, with twice as many men as women saying that global warming will never happen. One explanation is called the *system justification theory*, which it says that the more people benefit from the status quo, the more they are inclined to defend it. Conservative white men are the people who have benefitted from the current socioeconomic industrial setup most, and therefore are the ones who want to maintain it most. People are also more likely to ignore risks if they benefit from them. Other studies show that those benefiting from the current economic structure display less empathy to current and future victims of a threat (and in general women score higher on measures of empathy than men). And finally "being in denial" is one way of coping with a great threat, so much so that the phrase is in common usage.

So we have a picture whereby a large group of people has an unconscious motive for believing without question what others tell them. You have another much smaller group of people telling them what they want to hear. That's most of the people.

Then there are a few highly knowledgeable people on both sides who believe vehemently that they are right and have difficulty in understanding why experts on the other side don't agree with them and come to the same conclusions.

Given the mass of evidence, some sceptics resort to proclaiming that there is a conspiracy to promote the fallacious idea of anthropogenic climate change and hide the truth. They say that there are careers to be made in climate change science; that all the grant money is in supporting the establishment position, and researchers need grants to advance their careers; and even that the changes necessary to slow down climate change are tools to bludgeon the people and keep them down. Why do people believe in conspiracies? Of course conspiracy theories vary in their plausibility: I wouldn't be wholly surprised if it turned out that there was a conspiracy to assassinate President John F. Kennedy and cover up the truth, but would be very surprised indeed if the NASA moon landings had been faked. Climate change science as a conspiracy falls somewhere between these extremes. There has been controversial research that claims that ACC sceptics are more likely to believe in other conspiracy theories, but this research is controversial, to the extent that one paper on the subject was subsequently retracted by the publisher. Of course controversial does not mean wrong.

There are other factors that affect people's readiness to accept global warming. Our personality affects belief, but so does our state. We often do not know why we act as we do, and small things can affect behaviour. People are more likely to say they believe that global warming is happening if they are hot. How fickle we are. A recent study showed that, as ever, liberals express a significantly higher belief in global warming, but belief by both groups increased by about 1 point, on a 10-point scale, if they were sitting in a hot (27.2°C) compared with average (22.8°C) room. It seems that when you are hot, it gets easier to imagine a world that is suffering the effects of global warming, and that increases your belief in global warming. When it is hot, it may also become easier to think about heat conceptually, but that conceptual ease does not seem to translate into changes in beliefs about global warming.

This work also suggests that when you want to try to persuade someone about the importance of an issue whose effects won't be felt for years to come, it is important to try to make the long-term consequences feel as vivid as possible. Thus, documentaries like Al Gore's *An Inconvenient Truth* may be most effective because they provide clear images of what might happen to the earth as temperatures rise.

5

WEATHER AND SOCIETY

CLIMATE AND SOCIETY

Climate affects many types of individual differences, including personality and intelligence. Does it have wider cultural influences? Classical thinkers from Hippocrates to Montesquieu thought so. Hippocrates (c. 460–370 BCE) astutely believed that climate affected the preponderance of different types of diseases, which would have wider cultural consequences. He can hardly be blamed if the details were wrong, given the pre-scientific thinking of the time, but he had the right idea. Montesquieu (1689–1755) believed that certain climates were preferable to others: climates that were too extreme would hinder the development of more advanced cultures; he, a Frenchman, believed that the temperate climate of France was best. Those living in cold climates were likely to be overly formal and cold in their emotions, while those living in hot climates tended to being hot-headed.

These thinkers have modern successors. The management scientist and economist Philip M. Parker, in his books *Climatic Effects on Individual, Social and Economic Behavior* (1995) and *Physioeconomics: The Basis for Long-Run Economic Growth* (2000), explains the equatorial paradox, the phenomenon that a country's latitude explains nearly three quarters of the variation in per capita income between countries, in climatic terms. He advocates the idea that humans evolved in the tropics, and as they spread further north and south, away from equatorial regions, they had to master new skills to stay alive and later to produce goods. Eventually regions with less pleasant climates, such as North-western Europe, came to have a higher GDP than regions closer to where we evolved. One problem with this sort of view is that humans spread out of Africa a long time ago, and have had plenty of time to adjust. Another is that it isn't immediately obvious that the climate of France, say, is so much less pleasant than the climate of the savannah.

Human cultural evolution is marked by two great revolutions. The agricultural revolution began around 12,000 years ago in the Fertile Crescent between the Nile, Tigris, and Euphrates Rivers. It marked the end of the Neolithic (stone) age and the beginning of the bronze age, marking the end of hunter-gatherer societies, and the domestication of animals, the cultivation of crops, the stratification of societies, and the development of cities. It was possible only because the climate was clement enough for farming to be relatively easy. Without an appropriate climate, we would not be here. Others have gone further and argued that climatic changes were the driving force of agriculturalisation. A relatively early idea, proposed by V. Gordon Childe in his 1928 book Man Makes Himself, was that changes in the earth's climate led to the main path of rain-bearing Atlantic depressions shifting northwards, leading to a drier climate with hunter-gatherer communities contracting to oases, where they were forced into close proximity with other animals; however, modern climate studies suggest that the climate in the Fertile Crescent was getting wetter around this time, not drier. But perhaps this increased rainfall was a driving factor? It does seem far too much of a coincidence that the revolution occurred at the end of the last glacial period and the beginning of the current geological epoch, the Holocene. The climate became warmer and more stable, and was also marked by many extinctions of larger mammals previously hunted by the hunter-gatherers. So climate was at least one major driver of our cultural evolution.

The industrial revolution of course began in Britain and spread first through North-western Europe. There are many reasons for this monumental development, including the availability of natural resources in Britain, navigable and usable waterways, and a merchant society ready to invest in science, technology, and industry. The British art historian Dan Cruickshank has even suggested that the British devotion to tea played a part, because it meant boiling water and thereby killing waterborne pathogens, such as typhoid and cholera, and enabling the population to be sustainable and even grow when forced together in densely populated cities. Certainly plenty of water and a climate amenable to agricultural development that could support a growing workforce were also important. The British weather might not have been as central to the industrial revolution as climate change was to the agricultural revolution, but it played some role.

Van de Vliert, whose work on climate and intelligence we met in Chapter 1, argues that climate today plays a role in shaping the form of contemporary society. In 2013 he proposed that climate influences the type of government people get. Very hot and very cold climates are more demanding of resources to overcome the hostile environment. Individual liberty is lowest in poor populations that are perpetually threatened by demanding climates, intermediate in populations comforted by undemanding temperate climates irrespective of income per head, and highest in rich populations challenged by a demanding climate (but not overwhelmed by it). A repressive regime thrives on poverty and hot weather, an idea supported by a survey of 174 countries. Human freedoms (from want, from fear, from discrimination, and of expression) are also determined by climate interacting with income. Van de Vliert also found a similar pattern within the US, where there is a strong north-south temperature gradient; poverty tends to be higher in hot southern states, but not always (think of southern California). If you have plenty of money, you can pay your way out of most environmental unpleasantries. Political riots occur more frequently in warm countries, after controlling for effects of population size and the levels of socioeconomic development; from 1948 to 1964, the frequency of coups, assassinations, terrorism, guerrilla wars, and revolts varied with mean annual temperature, with violent events occurring more in warm climates (with an annual mean temperature of around 24°C). The numbers tail off when it gets much hotter; presumably the people are too hot to revolt. As a case study Tuvalu is one of the hottest countries in the world, with an annual mean temperature of 28°C, but is a parliamentary democracy where most human rights are respected, with freedom of the press, protection for minorities, and a low rate of crime.

These effects are moderated by the cultural dimension of masculinity – how macho the men are in a society – and hot blood comes with hot climates. Even the word "macho" comes from Mexican Spanish, with the macho man being aggressive, tough, independent, aggressive, competitive, and dominant; what a contrast from the metrosexual man of the colder climate of Northern Europe.

Many poorer populations cope with more demanding winters or summers by adopting more collectivist means of agriculture. In a comparison of 15 Chinese provinces, collectivism was found to be weakest in provinces with temperate climates irrespective of income (e.g., Guangdong), a little more popular in higher-income provinces with demanding climates (e.g., Hunan), and most popular in the lowest-income provinces with demanding climates (e.g., Heilongjiang). Again we find the effects of climate interacting with economic considerations. A more complex model might examine why these economic differences arise, and once again climate will play a role.

The orientation of the continents determines how much land falls under different climate types. Africa and the Americas have a major axis running north-south, meaning that climate changes fairly rapidly as you move along their length. Eurasia, though, is oriented east-west, meaning that climate and temperature aren't so different as you navigate its primary axis. Jared Diamond has suggested that this east-west orientation gave Eurasia an advantage in technological development. It so happens that the climate of Europe isn't too extreme, so crops grow readily. An agricultural advance made in Germany is very likely to be useful in France, so the east-west orientation allows technology to develop more quickly.

The climate can have some surprising cultural consequences. Within Britain there was a marked change in literature with the

Norman Conquest. Prior to 1066, Anglo-Saxon literature was about winter, frost, snow, hardship, and a battle against the elements; Norman literature was about spring and sunshine, and showed the influence of the Mediterranean. And the Renaissance started in the warm, sunny Mediterranean, and the Enlightenment in temperate Europe – surely such revolutions are more likely to occur when people are freed from battling the elements and the yield from crops is relatively high?

Climate change and global warming will have the consequence of destabilising some nations and cultures that are currently stable, and increasing conflict over natural resources, such as water. Wealthier nations will be able to adapt better by essentially buying their way out of trouble. Of course if your country disappears there's little you can do. The Netherlands already faces a perpetual battle against the sea, but it's estimated that 46% of its population lives on land likely to be affected by rising sea levels as the ice caps melt. But at least the Netherlands is wealthy; many countries in southeast Asia, such as Bangladesh, Thailand, Myanmar, and Vietnam, face the same problem without the same resources. It's not quite all bad news because some poorer countries in Asia are predicted to benefit from climate change.

WATCHING THE WEATHER FORECAST

We mostly obtain our knowledge about the upcoming weather from radio and television weather forecasts. People say they're interested in the weather, and go out of their way to watch a forecast, yet several studies have reliably shown that people's memory for what they have just seen is abysmal. One study even showed that people couldn't recognise which of four simple summaries for their own area matched what they had just seen. Of course the format of the weather forecast has changed over the years, evolving from magnetic clouds that drop off at random intervals to swanky computer graphics, but there is no evidence that people's memories have improved correspondingly. Yet there isn't really anything special about the forecast; our memory for text is governed by several well-known psychological principles, and it just happens that many aspects of the traditional forecast ignore these principles.

It's surprising what doesn't help make recall any better. Surely a televised forecast will be remembered much better than a radio forecast? No, it isn't. Does seeing a presenter help? Not really. (Indeed some people find them distracting, focusing on their tie or hand movements when they should be paying attention to the expected minimum in Oxford that night.) Even the presence of maps has been shown to make surprisingly little difference.

Several features of the forecast make the material difficult to understand, yet it is possible to do something about all of them. One problem appears to be that people treat the forecast like nonsense material, and so don't get the usual facilitation we get from processing meaningful material. Most people also find the forecast too long, so later bits interfere with earlier. Being a weather fanatic I at first found this result difficult to believe: testing myself, I had near perfect recall for the lengthy seven-day forecast across the UK, but on informally testing others I confirmed this result, in that highly educated university lecturers stare at me, unable to remember accurately virtually anything of what they have just seen. Forecasts are often presented very quickly, with a fast speech rate and few pauses, as the presenter tries to cram in a lot of material, while we know slow speech and many pauses in appropriate places improve retention.

Most people who live in east Scotland are not bothered about what is likely to happen in Devon and Cornwall, yet they have to watch the material, which quickly interferes with what they might be interested in. However, studies in the US have shown that people are also poor at remembering local forecasts. We know that reading for a purpose leads to better memory, yet most people who watch the forecast express interest in the weather and have a particular goal in watching it (need I take my umbrella tomorrow?).

On the other hand most people find the amount of information presented in forecasts to be overwhelming, and the presenter to be a distraction. It is possible to improve memory by targeting and limiting the amount of information and graphics, getting rid of the presenter, and presenting short verbal summaries. Redundancy and explanation help: explaining that the north winds are coming all the way from the Arctic and therefore are going to give cold weather helps to tell a story.

People cope with being overwhelmed by trying to simplify, and focusing on key words. One study showed that listeners remember words like "rain", "frost", or "snow", but not immediate important qualifications like "it will snow heavily in the south in the afternoon". This finding helps explain why people believe weather forecasts are less reliable than they are – someone hearing this forecast and reflecting on it in the north in the morning will take a dim view of it.

Another reason that people feel overwhelmed is because forecasters understandably try to cram in as much as possible: they are usually allocated a few minutes between the end of one programme and the top of the hour. As a consequence they talk fast, at rates up to 250 words a minute. We find such rapid speech, particularly when we have difficulty understanding the content, very hard to process: listening or watching a weather forecast really is like listening to a foreign language. Slowing the speech rate down to a far more typical 150 words a minute, and inserting more pauses, improves comprehension and thus recall.

I think that forecasters may overestimate what people know, and tend to talk about the wrong things. People may be interested in the weather, but they don't actually know very much about it. So they see a forecast with isobars and fronts and most people have little idea what these are or why they're important. I haven't been able to find a single person away from weather conferences and weather newsgroups who knows what an occluded front is. They see numbers like −5°C or 26°C on a map and many people don't really know what they mean; they know −5°C is cold, but quite how cold, how unusual is it? Colour coding of maps (the deeper the blue for colder, oranges and reds for hot) is understood better by the non-expert.

The American psychologist Mary Hegarty and her colleagues have examined the comprehension of visual weather forecasts as a special case of understanding any complex visuospatial display. They too have concluded that most people know a bit about how the weather works, but not really enough to be able to make full use of the information presented in most forecasts. So people have the *declarative* knowledge that air pressure is important in predicting wind direction (more important than temperature, say), but don't have the *procedural* knowledge to be able to make use of that information. They know that areas of high and low pressure determine wind direction, but cannot say how, or predict it from the map (in the northern hemisphere the winds blow clockwise around an anticyclone; with just this information you can just look at a synoptic chart and predict quite well what the weather is going to be like). Designers of weather charts need to make the right things salient: there is no point cramming it with all types of information as though they are of equal importance. Things that enable people to make use of the chart should be most prominent. A correctly designed forecast will enhance comprehension and retention.

The weather forecast necessarily deals with uncertainty rather than the certainty we like. Given the current nature of weather forecasting, there is nothing we can do about that, but we can do something about the way experts talk about that uncertainty. People find statements such as "there's a chance of rain tomorrow" difficult to understand – what on earth does "a chance" mean? The American tradition of talking in terms of concrete numbers as probabilities – there's a one in two chance of snow tomorrow, there's a 40% chance of rain – is much clearer and easier to understand. A survey of American listeners found that concrete numbers were greatly preferred when talking about probabilities.

Those of you who don't know will be eager to learn what an occluded front is. Most people know that a front separates two masses of air, and circulates around areas of low pressure: a warm front brings a warmer air mass, and a cold front colder air. They are both marked by weather events such as wind and particularly rain. As the area of low pressure matures the cold front may overtake and combine with the warm front so that you have three masses of air interaction, with a wedge of the coldest air at the bottom. I bet you're all glad you asked.

IGNORING SEVERE WEATHER FORECASTS

If the upcoming weather is deemed severe enough, the British Met Office might issue a severe weather warning. These are colour-coded – essentially yellow means be aware, orange means be prepared, and red means take action (batten down the hatches and stay indoors, with the verbal warning cheerfully telling us that there is a RISK OF DEATH!). Warnings are meant to minimise disruption and save lives; if you decide to climb a mountain when a blizzard is forecast, you're asking for trouble. Strangely, though, many people do ignore them. They head off on the road when a warning has been issued for heavy snow, and seem surprised when they get stuck. Someone should have warned me.

Of course winter-time slipperiness is a considerable source of elevated road accident risk, especially in northern countries, such as Canada, Finland, and Sweden. However, adversity brings forth inge-nuity, and in snowy climates four-wheel drive, snow chains, and even winter tyres make transport feasible and safe – or, depending on the snow depth, at least safer. In Scotland I keep intending to fit winter tyres, but then I remember last year's mild, disruption-free winter, and it all seems too much trouble; and then I end up being snowed in for a week, living on tinned tuna.

People ignore warnings for many reasons, which is strange given that much research has shown strong effects of loss aversion, where we really don't like losing, and risk aversion, where we really don't like risking losing stuff (including our lives). People are also loath to attribute negative features to themselves (we think other people are successful because they're just lucky, but we succeed because we're clever and work hard and thoroughly deserve our success), so it should not be a surprise that we think that bad stuff only ever hap-pens to other people, and never to us.

Not everyone ignores weather warnings, though. One study showed that some people are more likely to check the conditions and take action before setting out. Those most likely to check are older people, those with little driving experience, women, and those planning on heading out on a longer trip, perhaps on an unfamiliar route. People like me, middle-aged men who think they have seen it all and what's all the fuss about anyway, are most likely to ignore the warnings – and pay the price, as I have discovered to my cost a few times in the past. Poor local conditions also make people check and think twice. People coming to Scotland drive around the Central Lowlands and find it difficult to believe that 100 miles up the Great North Road cars are being abandoned, roads have become impassable, and people have been snowed into their cars for days.

Even drivers who have bothered to find out about information often don't change their behaviour that much. They might cancel or change their travel plans, but curiously the knowledge of what is ahead doesn't make them change their driving behaviour that much. This lack of caution might be because drivers generally consider the road conditions to be better than forecast, except for when it's dark or getting dark.

Other people know there are warnings in effect, but society sends them a mixed message. People think they will be penalised by their employers, for example, if they don't turn up to work, and lose money, or they will lose out if they don't make a meeting or their children will lose out if they're not taken to school. And I have observed that people are right to be concerned: the weather warning and police are advising them not to drive, but their employer hasn't told them to stay away, and the schools remain open. And what exactly is an "essential" journey, anyway?

It could be that things are going to get worse. Online media are now replacing traditional radio and television forecasts, and some of these may not display the warnings with quite the same effect that forecasters standing in front of a screen might have. At the same time with global warming the weather might well be getting more extreme, with more frequent and more severe weather events to come.

Warnings should be as local and specific as possible. As soon as viewers are told that there is a chance of severe weather in the next 24 hours somewhere in the country, they switch off, often literally. In addition, general, vague warnings increase the number of *false positives*, where we are told something bad is going to happen, but it never comes to pass. If a medium is forever telling people that bad things are going to happen, but they never do, it is not surprising that people eventually come to ignore those warnings. One day, though, the forecaster isn't crying wolf, and the weather is going to get you, as I have discovered a few times, to my cost. When the weather is likely to impinge on our safety, the forecaster should be pointing at you, saying this means you now.

In spite of warnings and forecasts, we are often surprised by the weather, as the British psychologist Richard Wiseman points out. We have seen that our memory for forecasts can be very bad, and our memory for weather warnings might be similarly poor. Maybe the reason people end up stuck in their cars in the centre of huge snow drifts is because, unlike me, some haven't been studying the forecast every 15 minutes. How strange.

CULTURAL ICONS

There are songs written about it. Its constituents are routinely used in quiz questions across Britain. You can buy expensive posters and maps depicting it, for yourself or gift-wrapped. Some use it as an aid to getting to sleep. There is an uproar if anyone suggests dropping it, even though it is of practical use only to a very small proportion of the British population, and much of the information is easily available all the time online. It was played as part of the opening music to the 2012 Olympic Games in London. It's the BBC shipping forecast, and it's deeply embedded in the British culture. It's a cultural icon – the map and the names of the areas on it bring on nostalgia and a tear in the eye: Forties, Dogger, Thames, Wight, Fastnet, Trafalgar. An early version of it was introduced by Vice Admiral Robert FitzRoy in 1861 in response to shipping disasters. It was broadcast on the radio from near its beginning, and has shifted around stations following long-wave stations, and is currently found on long-wave BBC Radio 4; after the last programme finishes on Radio 4, Ronald Binge's classical light piece "Sailing By" is played, followed by the shipping forecast, in the same format, every night. How relaxing.

Other aspects of how the media treat the weather have become cultural icons. Although we have seen that many people will remember very little of the televised weather forecasts, they are likely to remember what the broadcasters were wearing, or particular turns of phrase, some of which will be repeated and bemoaned in the letters columns of the national papers. Weather forecast presenters are famous, even though they may speak only for a few minutes each day: in the UK the names Bert Foord, Bill Giles, Ian McCaskill, and others live on in cultural memory long after they stopped presenting. Some forecasters make it into songs – "John Kettley Is a Weatherman", by the Tribe of Toffs, made it to number 21 in the UK Singles Chart. Some make it into song: Michael Fish appeared in a dance routine with The Weather Girls, performing "It's Raining Men".

It's not just in the UK that weather people are icons. Many famous US stars started out presenting the weather, including David Letterman, Barbara Walters, and even Raquel Welch, in San Diego on KFMB in the late 1950s, although she was just Raquel Tajada then. In the US, we have James Spann, with his superb knowledge of storms and tornadoes, Jim Cantore of the Weather Channel, and Al Roker (of NBC's Today and Nightly News), who is in Guinness World Records for setting a new record of 34 hours in 2014 for a single uninterrupted live weather forecast (yes, there really is such a category).

One of the most famous television moments (which by chance I caught) was a lunchtime weather forecast on 15 October 1987 when Michael Fish coolly announced that he had been phoned up by a woman who had heard there was a hurricane on the way, but she wasn't to worry – there wouldn't be a hurricane. That night the worst gale in centuries hit southern Britain, causing devastation, leaving 18 people dead, and felling 15 million trees. Although Fish correctly stated that he was technically right, he came across, as he himself admitted, as a bit of an idiot, and was mocked in the press. The incident is still legendary in forecasting annals.

Why are forecasters so memorable when they are on the screen for so little time? Partly they are chosen to be distinctive: few will forget some of the foregoing when they have seen their forecasts. They go out of their way to be distinctive; Michael Fish wore jumpers depicting the weather, often knitted for him by viewers, that linger in the memory of television sartorial bad taste. And perhaps because often they are more memorable than the weather the forecasters are talking about. Some weather stations across the world turn their forecasts into novelty acts, something perhaps very deliberately sartorially prominent, with weather girls in bikinis – or less.

WHY DO WE DREAM OF A WHITE CHRISTMAS?

Some like it hot, some don't; some like snow, some don't. We've seen that there are large individual differences in our preference for types of weather, but these individual differences are not stable across our lives or even across a much shorter period of time. Lines in W.B. Yeats's poem *The Wheel* remind us that

In winter we want spring,
in spring we want summer,
in summer winter is best of all.

We are never happy. Snow is often highly disruptive; some will remember the press mania in February 1991 when the British railways ground to a halt, blaming "the wrong kind of snow" (although that phrase was coined by the media, the railways representative had talked about "a different kind of snow", which is just as bad). The snow, following an incursion of cold continental air, was very soft and powdery, getting in stuck in places where snow and water were most unwelcome. The "wrong kind of snow" has become legendary as a very lame excuse.

But most children love snow, because it is fun to play in and may lead to that happiest of events, the cancellation of school. Most weather observers also love snow. But at Christmas it seems that everyone loves snow. It is strange to be in southern California just before Christmas, where images of white landscapes could rarely be more out of place. Suddenly one of the most dreaded of phenomena becomes something everyone wants; in an ideal world, after safely completing the last-minute Christmas Eve shopping, the flakes would start falling, and we would wake up Christmas morning to a thick blanket of fresh white snow (but not disrupting electrical supplies, of course).

Where has this obsession with snow at Christmas come from? After all, in spite of the occasional curious Christmas card, snow is hardly part of the Christmas story. In North-western Europe snow is not that common at Christmas, because late December is still early winter. In London the probability of a White Christmas is about 5%, in Birmingham 15%, in Manchester about 15%, in Glasgow 35%, and in Aberdeen around 50%. Of course it all depends how we define "White Christmas"; in the UK the bookies legendarily pay out if a flake of snow falls on the roof of the local meteorological office, whereas the US adopts the much more common-sense definition of an inch of snow on the ground at observation time (usually 9 a.m.) on Christmas morning. According to this definition, "real" widespread White Christmases are rare even in southern Britain, happening in recent years in 2009 and 2004. Before that you have to go back to 1970. So many people have grown up never experiencing one of the things they most want. Perhaps we should all move to Duluth, Minnesota, or Fairbanks, Alaska, where the probability of there being snow on the ground on Christmas Day is close to 100%.

These days the media feed our frenzied desire for snow as we whip each other up into expectant frenzies. As a (very) amateur weather observer, the earliest I have been asked about whether we will have a White Christmas this year is August. It's the most common question I'm asked, along with "what will the weather be like on the day of my wedding in May next year?" Of course given the accuracy of long-range forecasting we can make only the most general of guesses a few weeks before, and these guesses are often notoriously wrong – who could forget the Met Office's prediction for a barbecue summer in 2009, with that summer then turning out to be one of the wettest on record? Similarly you can only start to get a real idea of what is going to happen a couple of weeks before Christmas, and even then a great deal can change. At the moment forecasts firm up about a week before the event.

Media of various sorts agitate our desire, and they also started it. The song "White Christmas", by Irving Berlin, first performed by Bing Crosby on Christmas Day 1941, and then in the movie *Holiday Inn* in 1942, is the bestselling single of all time, Crosby's version (or one of them; he produced many) selling over 100 million copies alone. The combination of nostalgia, the war, and the picture of Christmas it depicts is irresistible. Charles Dickens's book *The Pickwick Papers* of 1836 captured a wonderful image of a White Christmas, with Mr Pickwick and chums at Dingly Dell Manor, and reflected the fact that a White Christmas was much more common in the Little Ice Age that started in earnest in North-western Europe in the mid-seventeenth century, but was by Dickens's time just starting to come to an end (although it would linger). A White Christmas is the perfect example of *anemoia*, nostalgia for a time we never knew.

Perhaps, though, snow is just wonderful, and Christmas is the most wonderful time of the year. Our minds link these two beautiful things, and we end up wanting them to occur together.

HUMANS AND NATURE

A reasonable general conclusion is that there are effects of the weather on mood and behaviour, but they're very small and sometimes very specific. Our intuitions as to what is happening are often wrong. As with much of psychology, experiments have often ignored individual differences, and it is undoubtedly the case that some individuals are more susceptible to being affected by the weather than others. We don't really currently understand the basis of these individual differences.

It is perhaps disappointing that in spite of our strong beliefs about how the weather and our climate affect us, it is surprisingly difficult to find robust evidence for them having strong effects on behaviour. I think it is particularly surprising that even though we have these beliefs, they make little difference; while humans are frequently susceptible to all kinds of bias, belief about the weather does not figure on the list. And we do need a degree of hardiness: if our behaviour were easily influenced by every little thing around us, we'd never bring the dinner home.

There is one way in which both the weather and humans are similar: they're both very complicated. It is well known that the weather is a complex system, by which we know it is very sensitive to initial conditions. Very small changes in the starting conditions can lead to enormous differences later on, which is why we have the oft quoted metaphor of the flap of a single butterfly's wing in the Amazon basin being the difference between a nice sunny day and a devastating storm in the northern hemisphere a few days later. The world's weather system is a prototypical complex system; its complexity is what makes forecasting the weather so difficult. Human behaviour is another complex system; our behaviour at any one time is the result of the state of the world up to that point. Behaviour is influenced by genes and our environment. There are 23 chromosomes each containing thousands of genes; one estimate is that the total possible number of genetic combinations in humans is over 70,000,000,000,000 (70 trillion) – that's a huge number, and vastly greater than the number of humans who have ever lived (about 100 billion). But such numbers are tiny compared to the complexity of our environment and the number of alternative actions across history that have led to now. Our behaviour at any one time is extremely complicated and a bit unpredictable – just like the weather. The same sorts of tools are necessary to understanding complexity in both cases.

Perhaps we should stop worrying so much and just enjoy the weather. Paying attention to the weather – appreciating rain and snow, enjoying a vivid sunset or an interesting display of clouds – is one way of connecting with nature. Weather is always there, you don't have to travel to see it, and it's free. This is perhaps why artists so often make use of it. Weather plays an important role in art. Landscape paintings and photographs are defined by their lighting, and often clouds and lighting are the focus of the landscape. The paintings of J.M.W. Turner are almost exclusively about light and how clouds and the weather affect the light. The landscapes of Constable make great use of clouds to affect the lighting. It's been argued that the outer landscapes of Constable's art reflect the inner landscapes of his moods through clouds and skies; as he became depressed after the death of his wife, his skies became heavier and more threatening, the clouds greyer, and the lighting more foreboding. Look at how Nicolas Poussin used clouds to help tell the story depicted in his pictures; every cloud feels just right.

Modern life, particularly western modern life, has many risks, including stress and physical and mental illness. To give a particular example, many places have lost the night sky. Stars aren't just beautiful, but too much artificial light at the wrong time of day can be dangerous, a killer even. Exposure to artificial light at night reduces our level of melatonin, and leads to an increased number of cancers, metabolic dysfunction, and an increased incidence of mood disorders. High levels of outside artificial light increase the risk of breast cancer by 14% compared to women who live in the darkest areas. Night shift workers are at greatest risk.

Several studies have shown that restoring the link between us and nature would be good for us. Feeling connected to nature confers protection against these stresses and facilitates better physical health, better cognitive skills, and mental well-being. In particular those who appreciate nature tend to have a better mood, be more satisfied with life, and especially feel more energetic, when everything else is taken into account. Being grounded in nature makes you happier. So paying attention to the weather could make you physically healthier, cleverer, and happier.

What makes you feel connected? As you might expect, mere exposure to nature isn't that effective; as with anything, the more effort you put in to something, the more you get out of it. We find connection through some kind of meaning: for example, finding a scene beautiful; being emotionally moved by something; or relating something to our lives. Knowing about something, or being able to tick something off on a list (and I plead guilty here) doesn't have quite the same benefits.

Feeling connected to nature perhaps unsurprisingly provokes pro-environmental feelings and makes the individual more likely to be environmentally active, although of course the direction of causality is complex. Being involved in any kind of environmental work is likely to make you pay more attention to your environment, which in turn will encourage you to do more to protect it.

Many argue that we have an innate tendency to appreciate nature and to seek connections with the natural world. This idea is called the biophilia hypothesis, and was first proposed in 1984 by the American sociobiologist E. O. Wilson. Strictly speaking, biophilia implies affiliating with living things, but it is only a small step to focusing on natural processes in general. Paying attention to nature conferred an evolutionary benefit to our ancestors; knowing where the lions lived, where water was most likely to be found, and which herbs were poisonous and which were beneficial was self-evidently advantageous. It is not a big stretch to argue that knowledge of the weather is similarly of evolutionary benefit.

There is some evidence that appreciation of nature depends on children being exposed to it; leave it too late and we are much less likely to be able to feel connected to the natural world. This dependence on early exposure means that as the population becomes increasingly urban, as cities and towns continue to sprawl into the countryside, as towns and villages merge into one another, as digital devices become our preferred playthings, and as people fear to let their children roam unsupervised, the next generation will be even less connected with nature. If caring for nature depends on being exposed to it, people in the future might put less importance on the survival of other species, the environment, and climate. In the worst case, we might be raising children not with indifference instead of biophilia but with biophobia, a term coined by the American environmentalist David W. Orr.

My own (unremarkable) childhood on the edge of a city allowed me, alone or with my younger sister, to roam through woods, fields, country lanes, and marshes, seeking birds, animals, and insects, in a way that would be thought unthinkable by many today. I remember staring in awe at the stars, wondering what clouds and the wind were, and being impressed by the beauty of dew and frost on grass. I loved the sun, heavy rain, and particularly snow. My obsession with the weather emerged naturally from my childhood.

Our obsession with the weather is much more than simply perceived. Being obsessed with the weather has contributed to the survival of our species in the past; it can facilitate our well-being in the present; and if we do not continue to respect the power of weather and climate, then it might see our extinction in the near future.

FURTHER READING

This section gives pointers to key reading and some places to go next. Except where I think it is essential, or where that reference is the one best source in the area, I have tried to minimise the number of academic papers I mention. A full list, however, of all the academic papers consulted in writing this book can be found on my website at http://trevorharley.com/Psychology_books.html. If you think I have missed an important paper, or would like to make me aware of your research, or maybe think that I haven't given credit to something I should have done, please email me at trevor.harley@mac.com.

I like to think that this book explores new territory for the non-expert, so there isn't always a great deal of reading that would be easily comprehensible for someone without a psychology degree. Even an Internet search will primarily throw up academic papers. The exception of course is on climate change, where a search will generate more than an expert could reasonably read in a few lifetimes.

Alter, A. (2014). *Drunk tank pink: The subconscious forces that shape how we think, feel, and behave.* New York, NY: OneWorld Publications. This excellent book has a chapter on how weather affects us in small and big ways, and is a rich source of information for many of the topics in this book. Adam Alter boldly starts a section of his 2014 book by saying, "Sunshine dulls the mind to risk and thoughtfulness".

Ayton, P. (1988). Perceptions of broadcast weather forecasts. *Weather*, 43, 193–197. A good review of the design of weather forecasts.

Beattie, G. (2018). *The Psychology of climate change*, by Routledge, in this series. The literature on seasons and suicide is dispersed over several journals, and there is not as much of it as you might expect for such an important topic that is aimed at the lay reader.

Bedrosian, T. A., & Nelson, R. J. (2017). Timing of light exposure affects mood and brain circuits. *Translational Psychiatry, 7,* e1017. A recent review of the effects of artificial light.

Capaldi, A. C. A., Dopko, L. R. L., & Zelenski, J. M. (2014). The relationship between nature connectedness and happiness: A meta-analysis. *Frontiers in Psychology, 5,* 1–15. A meta-analysis, which pools the results of many studies, showing the extent to which nature connectedness affects our well-being.

Charry, J. M., & Hawkinshire, F. B. (1981). Effects of atmospheric electricity on some substrates of disordered social behavior. *Journal of Personality and Social Psychology, 41,* 185–197. The classic reference on the effects of positive ions on behaviour.

Cook, J., Oreskes, N., Doran, P. T., Anderegg, W. R. L., Verheggen, B., Maibach, E. W., . . . & Greens, S. A. (2016). Consensus on consensus: A synthesis of consensus estimates on human-caused global warming. *Environmental Research Letters, 11.* Retrieved from http://doi.org/10.1088/1748-9326/11/4/048002. For the study on consensus among weather researchers about humans being responsible for climate change.

Denissen, J. J. A., Butalid, L., Penke, L., & van Aken, M. A. G. (2008). The effects of weather on daily mood: A multilevel approach. *Emotion, 8,* 662–667. The largest, most recent study, which references all the other papers in the area of mood and cognition.

Diamond, J. (1997). *Guns, germs, and steel.* New York, NY: Norton. Diamond's masterpiece is a life-changing book, making a huge contribution to understanding why things are as they are. Climate plays a central role in his account.

Fox, K. (2014). *Watching the English: The hidden rules of English behaviour* (revised ed.). London: Hodder & Stoughton. A fascinating and much quoted book on much more than the weather.

Gore, A. (2006). *An inconvenient truth.* Paramount Classics. Former Vice President Al Gore's (2006) documentary movie is a very good place to start with climate change. It won two Academy Awards.

Harris, A. (2016). *Weatherland:Writers and artists under English skies.* London: Thame & Hudson. A survey of how culture interprets the weather, and how weather influences art.

Keller, M. C., Fredrickson, B. L., Ybarra, O., Côté, S., Johnson, K., Mikels, J., . . . & Wager, T. (2005). A warm heart and a clear head: The contingent effects of weather on mood and cognition. *Psychological Science, 16,* 724–731. Another important study in the area of weather and mood. Both this paper and that by Denissen et al. are rich sources of references to further research in the area.

Klimstra, T. A., Frijns, T., Keijsers, L., Denissen, J. J. A., Raaijmakers, Q. A. W., van Aken, M. A. G., . . . & Meus, W. H. J. (2011). Come rain or come shine: Individual differences in how weather affects mood. *Emotion, 11,* 1495–1499. An important academic paper on how individual differences moderate the way weather influences mood.

Lewandowsky, S., Cook, J., Oberauer, K., Brophy, S., Lloyd, E. A., & Marriott, M. (2015). Recurrent fury: Conspiratorial discourse in the blogosphere triggered by research on the role of conspiracist ideation in climate denial. *Journal of Social and Political Psychology, 3,* 142–178. The use of the word "conspiracy" when talking about climate change is unsurprisingly highly controversial. In 2013 the British psychologist Stephan Lewandowsky published a paper called "Recursive Fury", describing the reaction of climate change sceptics to an earlier paper of his. Following complaints that the paper smeared sceptics by associating them with conspiracy theorists, the journal *Frontiers in Psychology* withdrew the paper, provoking yet another conspiracy, this time about freedom of expression – seen by others as how far can people be insulted in a free society.

Lomborg, B. (2001). *The skeptical environmentalist: Measuring the real state of the world.* Cambridge: Cambridge University Press. A classic reference for a very different, more sceptical view on humanity's effect on the environment (not just global warming), compared with Gore's.

Lynn, R. (2015). *Race differences in intelligence: An evolutionary analysis* (revised ed.). Washington, DC: Washington Summit Publishers. Richard Lynn's work on regional differences in IQ is controversial, but then so is almost anything on IQ, particularly if it involves race. You only have to look at the reviews on an online store such as Amazon to see what feelings this type of work promotes, which is hardly surprising when many consider such research to be politically motivated.

Mann, M. E. (2014). *The hockey stick and the climate wars.* New York, NY: Columbia University Press. In reply to the sceptics mentioned here.

Montford, A. W. (2010). *The hockey stick illusion.* London: Stacey International. More recent sceptical popular works on climate change. The term *hockey stick* refers to the shape of the graph of average world temperature plotted against time (over hundreds of years), supposedly showing a dramatic increase in recent years.

Rindermann, H. (2007). The g-factor of international cognitive ability comparisons: The homogeneity of results in PISA, TIMSS, PIRLS, and IQ-tests across nations. *European Journal of Personality, 21,* 667–706. A major research article with comments by other experts in the area.

Rosenthal, N. E. (2012). *Winter blues: Everything you need to know to beat seasonal affect disorder* (4th ed.). New York, NY: Guilford Press. The best-known and most popular book on seasonal affect disorder. It is regularly revised with the latest research.

Taylor, P. (2009). *Chill: A reassessment of global warming theory.* Forest Row, East Sussex: Clairview Books. Taylor argues that rather than worrying about global warming, we should be more concerned about global cooling and a return to the ice age. This view was very popular in the 1970s, but much less so now.

Wagenaar, W. A., & Visser, J. G. (1979). The weather forecast under the weather. *Ergonomics, 22,* 909–917. One of the classic studies of our memory for radio and televised weather forecasts.

Wilson, E. O. (1984). *Biophilia.* Cambridge, MA: Harvard University Press. There has recently been a deluge of research on the ways in which contact with nature facilitates mental and physical well-being. This book is one of the classics in the area.

Printed in the United States
by Baker & Taylor Publisher Services